M000211540

ONE
TIN
BAKES
EASY

Edd Kimber

TO MIKE AND WESLEY

ONE TIN BAKES EASY

Edd Kimber
@THEBOYWHOBAKES

PHOTOGRAPHY BY EDD KIMBER

KYLE BOOKS

An Hachette UK Company
www.hachette.co.uk

First published in Great Britain in 2021 by
Kyle Books, an imprint of Octopus Publishing Group Limited
Carmelite House
50 Victoria Embankment
London EC4Y 0DZ
www.kylebooks.co.uk

ISBN: 978 0 85783 978 7

Text copyright 2021 © Edd Kimber
Design and layout copyright 2021 © Kyle Books

Distributed in the US by Hachette Book Group, 1290 Avenue of the Americas,
4th and 5th Floors, New York, NY 10104

Distributed in Canada by Canadian Manda Group, 664 Annette St., Toronto,
Ontario, Canada M6S 2C8

Edd Kimber is hereby identified as the author of this work in accordance with
Section 77 of the Copyright, Designs and Patents Act 1988.

All rights reserved. No part of this work may be reproduced or utilised in any
form or by any means, electronic or mechanical, including photocopying,
recording or by any information storage and retrieval system, without the prior
written permission of the publisher.

Publishing Director: Judith Hannam
Publisher: Joanna Copestick
Senior Commissioning Editor: Louise McKeever
Design: Evi-O. Studio | Evi O. & Kait Polkinghorne
Photography & Food Styling: Edd Kimber*
Production: Emily Noto

*Image on page 175 © Simon Kimber

A Cataloguing in Publication record for this title is available
from the British Library

Printed and bound in China

10 9 8 7 6 5 4 3 2 1

INTRODUCTION

Easy does not have to mean boring. In fact, a recipe that requires little equipment or only a few ingredients can be just as exciting or delicious as something more complicated. It also has the advantage of not taking a lot of time. This came home to me in 2020, the year that Covid 19 forced itself onto the world and we all went into lockdown. Suddenly being stuck indoors meant I had time for projects, time to experiment, and I relished the opportunity to spend days in the kitchen playing around with new ideas and new recipes. Quickly, though, I found that being stuck at home changed the way I looked at baking, at least for a while. I wanted instant gratification. I craved easy baking.

In this book I want to show you how to bake incredible cakes, moreish cookies and delectable desserts that you'll want to curl up with in front of a fire, and without breaking a sweat or making a disaster zone out of your kitchen. There are recipes that need just five ingredients, one bowl cakes that you'll have in the oven within minutes, no bake recipes for when you can't even be bothered to turn on the oven, cookie recipes to feed a crowd, and desserts for when comfort is the order of the day. In each chapter there are also recipes for gluten-free and vegan baking, so no matter who you are baking for, you'll always find a recipe to suit.

Why, you might ask, does the book cater for such a mixture of dietary preferences? The simple answer is choice and popularity. Over the last few years, the demand for gluten-free and vegan options has grown incredibly quickly, and while I am neither a vegan nor on a gluten-free diet, many of my friends are, and having an arsenal of recipes that I can make for anyone is incredibly useful. It's also because I am in neither of those camps that I have tried to limit the number of specialist ingredients needed. Most of the items required in this book will be familiar to you, and widely available. The small handful of replacement ingredients I call for, such as vegan eggs and gluten-free flour, are also easy to find these days.

Baking is very often about sharing and celebrating with others, and the recipes in this book, and in the original *One Tin Bakes* for that matter, were written with those moments in mind. Building on the successful formula of baking everything in the same 23 x 33cm (9 x 13in) tin, I have also included a guide for those times when you want to bake a smaller version for just a few people, or for those occasions when you are baking just for yourself (and why not?).

I have written about baking for over ten years, and while my enjoyment and fascination with the subject have never diminished, the recent times of isolation and stress, of lockdowns and restriction, have once again shown me that baking can be more than the end product we eat – it can be the joy, the excitement, the bright spot in our day, even if right now we need things simple and quick.

THE BASICS

THE TIN

When it comes to choosing the right baking tin for the recipes in this book, there are a few things to bear in mind. I tested many brands and types of 23 x 33cm (9 x 13in) tin and it quickly became apparent that they're far from being all the same – some are a little wider, some a little shorter. To account for these variations, it's crucial to use a tin that is at least 5cm (2in) deep and all the recipes will fit without any issues.

With this style of tin you also have a choice between metal, glass and ceramic, plus a variety of different finishes, including enamel and non-stick. For the broad range of recipes in this book I recommend a good-quality aluminium tin, a classic bakeware choice that will happily stand the test of time. Apart from being lightweight and easy to look after, the metal is a good conductor of heat and helps to ensure even browning. My favourite version comes from Nordic Ware, one of the oldest and best bakeware manufacturers in the world. The one style I would avoid is a non-stick tin with a dark or black coating. These tins are also prone to getting scratched, but, even worse, distribute heat more quickly and often unevenly. This can lead to recipes browning too fast and sometimes even burning. If you already own such a tin, be aware of this drawback and either slightly reduce the oven temperature or check for doneness a few minutes before the stipulated time.

HOW TO LINE THE TIN

There are four main methods of preparing the tin:

1. Simply greasing the tin without a parchment paper lining – used for recipes served straight from the tin.

2. Lining the base with parchment paper – used for recipes that are portioned inside the tin, as the parchment helps to prevent the base from sticking.

3. Using a strip of parchment paper that overhangs the long sides of the tin and is held in place with metal binder or bulldog clips – used like a sling when a cake needs to be lifted from the tin after baking.

4. Lining the whole tin with a large single sheet of parchment paper or foil that fully covers both base and sides – used when the recipe has a tendency to stick to the sides, making it harder to remove.

1

2

3

4

SCALING DOWN

When the first *One Tin Bakes* was sent to the printer, it happened to coincide with finding ourselves in the midst of a global pandemic. Baking was used by many people, myself included, as a form of comfort, a type of self-care, but because we couldn't see friends and family in the usual way, we couldn't share our baking. We were baking for a crowd when only a few were able to enjoy it.

While I hope the world is back to normal by the time this book is released, I am including some general guidance on making smaller versions of the recipes that appear in this book, which can also be applied to those in the first for that matter. When using the smaller tins mentioned below, the baking times should be altered as suggested, but these are only a rough guide, so don't forget to check for doneness by using the visual clues given in the recipe as well.

HALF BATCHES	Half batches of *One Tin Bakes* recipes generally work well in a square 20 x 20cm (8 x 8in) tin, as long as it is at least 5cm (2in) deep. They will generally need about 5–10 minutes less baking time than a full batch of the recipe.
QUARTER BATCHES	Quarter-sized batches of the recipes usually work well in a 23 x 12.5cm (9 x 5in) loaf tin, and will generally need 10–15 minutes less baking than a full batch of the recipe.

GLUTEN-FREE NOTES

FLOUR AND SPECIALITY INGREDIENTS

Gluten-free baking can be daunting, as gluten helps to hold recipes together,and the gluten that is developed when using wheat flour is hard to replicate. People on a gluten-free diet commonly have a plethora of speciality ingredients on hand to create custom flour blends. But if you're not gluten-free and are simply baking for someone who is, you might not want to stock up on ingredients you'll rarely use.

To keep things simple, I generally use a shop-bought gluten-free flour, which eliminates the need for multiple bags of magic powders and potions. I tested my recipes with two of the leading brands of gluten-free flour – Doves Farm Organic Gluten-Free Plain (all-purpose) Flour and Bob's Red Mill Gluten-Free 1 to 1 Baking Flour. These are both blends of different grains, the main difference being that Bob's Red Mill contains xanthan gum and Doves Farm does not. Xanthan gum is a binding agent that helps prevent gluten-free baking from becoming crumbly and falling apart. In my recipes I include it when needed, giving the option to leave it out if using a flour that already includes it. While xanthan might sound like something from a chemistry lesson, it's just a powder, very similar to baking powder, and now widely available in supermarkets.

VEGAN NOTES

VEGAN EGGS

A handful of the vegan recipes that appear in this book require 'vegan eggs', which can be made from ground flaxseed or ground psyllium husks. Flaxseeds are easier to find, being available in most large supermarkets, but I prefer the egg made with psyllium husks, which can very easily be found in healthfood stores and online. Both ingredients have a very long shelf life.

The two types of egg are actually gels that are very easy to make (see below). The seeds or husks are generally mixed with water, but other liquids can be used if you want a specific flavour, as in the Lemon and Lime Courgette Cake (see page 45). My preference for psyllium is because I find it more effective, it has less flavour and makes a stronger gel than flax, so is great for making moist cakes and desserts.

HOW TO MAKE VEGAN EGGS

1 VEGAN EGG = 1 LARGE CHICKEN'S EGG

Flaxseed and psyllium are just two of the ingredients from which vegan eggs can be made, and if you explore vegan baking in any detail, you'll find many others. To my mind, these two options work wonderfully in the recipes in this book.

FLAX EGG

1 tablespoon ground flaxseed

3 tablespoons water

PSYLLIUM EGG

1 teaspoon psyllium husks

3 tablespoons water

Put whichever ingredient you are using in a small bowl, mix in the water and set aside until it has thickened to the slightly gloopy texture of a whisked egg.

VEGAN CHOCOLATE

You'll notice in the vegan recipes involving chocolate that I use regular dark chocolate, which is because it should contain no dairy products and therefore tends to be vegan. It is worth checking the packaging, however, as some brands may contain traces of dairy and would not be classed as vegan.

I tend to favour dark chocolate when baking vegan as it is the simplest swap, but there is now a wide variety of vegan 'milk' and white chocolate available. Look out for chocolate made with nut milk powders, or even with oat milk. They're not always as creamy as the dairy alternative, but are a good option if you're not a dark chocolate fan.

VEGAN BUTTER

As with a lot of vegan ingredients, there is no real uniformity of style with vegan butter. The margarine types are spreadable straight from the tub, while the block types have a similar texture and appearance to dairy butter, but every brand is slightly different because it's made from different ingredients. When it comes to baking, and this book specifically, I keep things simple: the only vegan butter I use is the block type, as I find it a better across-the-board option. In the UK I choose Naturli', and in the US/Australia my choice is Miyoko's.

VEGAN AND GLUTEN-FREE PRODUCT WARNING

It is important to be aware that many ingredients you might expect to be vegan or gluten-free sometimes include additives that make them unsuitable. Puffed rice, for example, is made from rice, which is naturally gluten-free and vegan, so why would the cereal not be? Well, some brands add malt syrup, which may contain gluten, and some add vitamin D, which may be non-vegan in origin. It is always worth checking the packaging, just in case the product inside contains something you need to avoid. Fortunately, given the wide choice we have at supermarkets, there is generally an option that is suitable. In particular, look to own brand varieties, which I've found often fit the bill. One helpful development is that most brands of baking powder are now made with a gluten-free starch, such as rice flour, so I don't specify a gluten-free baking powder in the recipes. However, it is always worth checking the packaging, as one or two manufacturers still include wheat starch.

INGREDIENTS

BUTTER/FAT	For dairy-based recipes, I use butter that has at least an 82% butterfat content, and I choose unsalted because it allows me to control the salt level in a recipe myself; as you might have noticed, every brand of salted butter varies in its degree of saltiness. For vegan baking I use an unsalted block-style of vegan butter, and a variety of oils (olive, vegetable and coconut). When using coconut oil, you have a choice between refined and unrefined/virgin. Both types can be used in the recipes calling for coconut oil; the main difference is flavour – the unrefined oil has a pronounced coconut flavour, whereas the refined oil has a more neutral aroma and flavour. Where recipes call for a 'neutral' oil, you can use sunflower or regular vegetable oil (a blend of different oils). If you want added flavour, all recipes that call for oil can be made with olive oil. Rapeseed (canola) oil also works well for baking, but if you're in the UK, I recommend avoiding cold-pressed varieties, as the oil can have a strong flavour that you might not want in your baking.
CREAM	I use mainly double cream, which is a dairy product with a fat content of about 48%. In the US and Canada the nearest equivalent is heavy or whipping cream. If in doubt, use the cream with a fat content nearest to the UK product.

CHOCOLATE & COCOA POWDER

When recipes call for chocolate with a certain percentage of cocoa solids it is because it has an effect on the overall flavour and texture. In such cases, I tend to use a chocolate containing between 60% and 75% cocoa solids. Where chocolate is listed with no specification, it is generally being used as a 'mix-in', so you can use whichever type you prefer.

All the cocoa powder used in this book should be Dutch process, which means it has been treated to reduce its acidity and give it a richer flavour. This type is the norm in Europe, especially in supermarkets, but in the US, both Dutch process and natural cocoa are widely available. Wherever you live, I recommend buying cocoa powder with the words 'Dutch process' or maybe 'treated with an alkali process' somewhere on the packaging. It is also possible to tell the difference from the colour: natural cocoa tends to have a dusty, almost grey tint to it, whereas Dutched cocoa ranges from rich red browns through to deep black. If you like the colour and flavour of black cocoa, it can be used in any of the recipes calling for cocoa powder, as it is another style of Dutched cocoa. Whatever you buy, do ensure it is unsweetened.

COCONUT CREAM

As there are numerous vegan recipes in this book, I use a lot of coconut cream – the canned variety, not the dairy milk alternative that comes in cartons. When it is used to replace whipped cream, it is a good idea to refrigerate the can overnight so that the coconut water separates from the thicker coconut cream. If the recipe instructs you to, discard the water and use just the cream. If there is no instruction to this effect, use the whole contents of the can.

EGGS

All the recipes in this book use large eggs, as defined by the UK and EU, which means they weigh 63–73g. The equivalent in the US, Canada and Australia is generally extra large.

SALT

I generally use two types of salt: fine sea salt and flaked sea salt. I avoid table salt, as the flavour is poor and leaves an acrid aftertaste. Fine sea salt is best for seasoning batters and doughs because it dissolves easily, while flaked sea salt is great for sprinkling over at the end, as I sometimes do with cookies, to add a little texture and a pop of saltiness. If you want to reduce the salt used in the recipes, feel free, but be aware that they may end up tasting a little bland. Remember that salt is not just for seasoning savoury dishes – it helps to bring out the flavours in baked goods too.

SUGAR

The recipes in this book use a variety of sugars, but the one I use most is white caster sugar, a fine-grained variety, known as superfine in the US. I understand that this can be difficult to get hold of in some places overseas, so the best advice I can give is to use the finest-grained sugar you can buy, whether that be superfine or regular granulated. The other sugar I use a lot is light brown sugar, especially unrefined versions, as the molasses content is higher and the flavour tends to be deeper. This type often goes by the name light brown muscovado sugar.

When it comes to vegan baking, sugar is not something you might have thought would need consideration. The raw product is naturally vegan, but variations in processing mean that not all brands are vegan. In the UK, most of the major sugar brands are vegan-inclusive, but please check the packaging of whatever you buy to ensure it is certified vegan; this is especially important for icing (powdered) sugar. In the US, things are a little more complicated, as some manufacturers produce the same branded product in different factories, and trace elements of non-vegan products may cross-contaminate in one place but not another. The only way around this problem is to look for sugars that are USDA-certified organic, as these are always vegan.

VANILLA

Vanilla is to bakers what salt and pepper are to cooks – it's a seasoning to add another layer of flavour. Over the last few years, the price of vanilla has rocketed, so while a vanilla pod (bean) is a wonderful treat occasionally, I rely more on vanilla extract and vanilla bean paste, as they are more affordable.

ONE BOWL & ALL IN ONE CAKES

MARBLE CAKE

SERVES 12–15

Not just chocolate and not just vanilla, this marble cake is the best of both worlds and a throwback to childhood. It's really easy to make – in fact far easier than its impressive appearance would lead you to think – and such a crowd-pleaser that it's a great recipe to have in your repertoire. If you want an alternative to the buttercream topping, a simple chocolate ganache would be a great option.

225g (8oz/2 sticks) very soft unsalted butter, plus extra for greasing

400g (14oz/3 cups) gluten-free plain (all-purpose) flour

1½ teaspoons xanthan gum (omit if your flour blend already includes it)

350g (12oz/1¾ cups) caster (superfine) sugar

3 teaspoons baking powder

1 teaspoon fine sea salt

4 tablespoons neutral-tasting oil

5 large eggs

240ml (8½fl oz/1 cup) sour cream

2 teaspoons vanilla extract

4 tablespoons cocoa powder

1 tablespoon whole milk

FOR THE BUTTERCREAM

200g (7oz/1¾ sticks) unsalted butter, at room temperature

400g (14oz/3⅓ cups) icing (powdered) sugar

1 teaspoon vanilla bean paste

6 tablespoons double (heavy) cream

70g (2½oz) white chocolate, melted and cooled

70g (2½oz) dark chocolate, melted and cooled

3 tablespoons cocoa powder

Preheat the oven to 180°C (160°C Fan) 350°F, Gas Mark 4. Lightly grease your 23 x 33cm (9 x 13in) baking tin and line with a strip of parchment paper that overhangs the long sides, securing it in place with metal clips.

Place the flour in a large bowl, add the xanthan gum (if using), the sugar, baking powder and salt and whisk to combine. Add the butter, oil, eggs, sour cream and vanilla and beat together until a smooth batter forms. Pour half the batter into a separate bowl and add the cocoa powder and milk. Mix until fully combined.

Dollop large spoonfuls of each batter into the prepared tin, alternating them to create a chequered effect. (I find triggered ice-cream scoops make light work of this job, but using a couple of large spoons also works well.)

With a chopstick or pointed knife, lightly swirl the batters together to create a marbled effect, while ensuring the two colours remain nice and defined.

Bake for 40 minutes, or until the cake springs back to a light touch and is just coming away from the sides of the tin. Leave to cool for 20 minutes before using the parchment paper to lift onto a wire rack to cool completely.

For the buttercream, beat the butter in a large bowl until soft and creamy. Add the icing sugar a few spoonfuls at a time, beating well between each addition. When incorporated, beat the buttercream with an electric mixer on a high speed for 5–10 minutes, or until very light and fluffy. Add the vanilla and 4 tablespoons of the cream and beat to combine.

Scoop half the buttercream into a clean bowl and mix in the white chocolate. Add the dark chocolate, cocoa powder and remaining 2 tablespoons cream to the other bowl and mix well. Dollop the two lots of buttercream randomly over the cake, then swirl and spread them to create a marbled effect.

Stored in a sealed container, this will keep for 2–3 days.

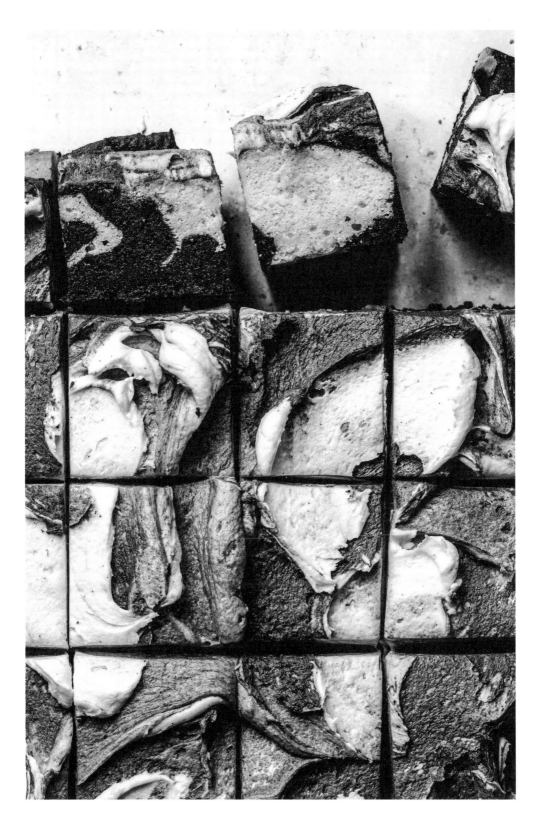

GRAPEFRUIT POPPY SEED SNACK CAKE

SERVES 12–15

Lemon poppy seed cake is an absolute classic, but why does no other citrus flavour get a look in? Why not blood orange or lime? For this version I have gone with grapefruit, as its slight bitterness counters the sweetness of the cake. Made with ground almonds and cornmeal, this is a moist cake that happily keeps for a few days, and is a delicious snack cake, not too sweet, and perfect for an elevenses treat.

225g (8oz/2 sticks) very soft unsalted butter, plus extra for greasing

300g (10½oz/1½ cups) caster (superfine) sugar

Zest of 2 pink grapefruit

225g (8oz/2⅓ cups) ground almonds

225g (8oz/1½ cups) fine cornmeal

4 tablespoons poppy seeds, plus extra for sprinkling

¾ teaspoon baking powder

6 large eggs

2 teaspoons vanilla extract

Pink grapefruit segments, to serve

FOR THE GLAZE

140g (5oz/⅔ cup) cream cheese, at room temperature

70g (2½oz/5 tablespoons) soft unsalted butter

1 teaspoon vanilla bean paste or extract

240g (8½oz/2 cups) icing (powdered) sugar

Juice of 1 pink grapefruit

Preheat the oven to 180°C (160°C Fan) 350°F, Gas Mark 4. Lightly grease your 23 x 33cm (9 x 13in) baking tin and line with a strip of parchment paper that overhangs the long sides, securing it in place with metal clips.

Put the sugar and zest into a large bowl and rub together with your fingers until the mixture resembles wet sand. (The rubbing helps to bring out the oils in the zest, increasing the flavour.) Add the remaining cake ingredients, except for the grapefruit segments, and beat with an electric mixer or wooden spoon until a smooth batter forms. Pour the batter into the prepared tin and spread evenly.

Bake for 30–35 minutes, or until a skewer inserted in the middle of the cake comes out clean. Leave to cool in the tin for 15 minutes before using the parchment paper to lift the cake onto a wire rack to cool completely.

For the glaze, beat the cream cheese and butter together in a bowl until smooth. Add the vanilla bean paste and icing sugar and beat again until smooth. Mix in just enough grapefruit juice to give a thick but just pourable glaze. Pour on top of the cooled cake and spread evenly.

To serve, top the cake with some fresh grapefruit segments and a sprinkling of poppy seeds.

If stored in a sealed container, the glazed cake will keep for 3–4 days, but add the fresh fruit and sprinkled poppy seeds just before serving.

RHUBARB AND CARDAMOM CAKE WITH BROWN BUTTER STREUSEL

SERVES 12

In some ways this simple one bowl cake resembles a classic coffee cake, but in place of the traditional cinnamon and brown sugar swirl is a wonderfully fragrant layer of rhubarb. The streusel topping has also had a makeover, being flavoured here with a touch of cardamom, brown sugar and brown butter. Made with tender forced rhubarb, this would brighten up any cold winter's day.

250g (9oz/1 cup + 2 tablespoons) very soft unsalted butter, plus extra for greasing

375g (13¼oz/3 cups) plain (all-purpose) flour

250g (9oz/1¼ cups) caster (superfine) sugar

4 teaspoons baking powder

½ teaspoon fine sea salt

4 large eggs

1 teaspoon vanilla extract

150ml (5fl oz/½ cup + 2 tablespoons) sour cream

300g (10½oz) rhubarb, cut into 2cm (¾in) pieces

Icing (powdered) sugar, for dusting

FOR THE STREUSEL

100g (3½oz/7 tablespoons) unsalted butter, diced

125g (4½oz/1 cup) plain (all-purpose) flour

70g (2½oz/⅓ cup) light brown sugar

Pinch of salt

1 teaspoon ground cardamom

As this cake comes together very quickly, make the streusel an hour before the batter so it has plenty of time to chill. Place the butter in a small saucepan over a medium heat until browned: at first it will melt, then sizzle and splatter (this is the water separating out and evaporating), and eventually it will foam. As it foams, you'll see golden brown flecks start to appear, and this is browned butter. As the butter is browning, mix the remaining streusel ingredients in a small bowl. When the butter is browned, pour it into the bowl of dry ingredients and mix to form a crumbly dough. Refrigerate for 1 hour or until firm.

Preheat the oven to 180ºC (160ºC Fan) 350ºF, Gas Mark 4. Lightly grease your 23 x 33cm (9 x 13in) baking tin and line it with a strip of parchment paper that overhangs the long sides, securing it in place with metal clips.

To make the cake, place the flour, sugar, baking powder and salt in a large bowl and whisk to combine. For one bowl cakes it is important that the butter is very soft, otherwise you'll end up mixing for far too long and the cake will become tough. Add the butter, eggs, vanilla and sour cream and mix just until a batter forms. Pour into the prepared tin and spread evenly, then scatter over the rhubarb pieces. Remove the streusel from the refrigerator, break into small pieces and sprinkle over the cake.

Bake for about 50 minutes, or until a skewer inserted in the middle of the cake comes out clean. Leave to cool in the tin for 20 minutes before using the parchment paper to lift the cake onto a wire rack to cool completely. Dust with a little icing sugar and serve.

If stored in a sealed container, this cake will keep for about 3 days.

ESPRESSO CARAMEL CAKE

SERVES 12

The traditional British coffee-and-walnut-style cake isn't for me, as I generally find it too sweet and the coffee flavour always tastes artificial because it's made with a bitter extract instead of the real deal. This simple sheet cake contains lots of espresso to create a genuine coffee kick, and the quick whipped caramel cream frosting is the perfect finishing touch.

170g (6oz/1½ sticks) very soft unsalted butter, plus extra for greasing

320g (11¼oz/2½ cups + 1 tablespoon) plain (all-purpose) flour

3 teaspoons baking powder

½ teaspoon fine sea salt

175g (6oz/¾ cup + 2 tablespoons) caster (superfine) sugar

175g (6oz/¾ cup + 2 teaspoons) light brown sugar

3 large eggs

2 teaspoons vanilla extract

100ml (3½fl oz/⅓ cup + 4 teaspoons) cold espresso or very strong black coffee

75ml (2¾fl oz/5 tablespoons) sour cream

Flaked sea salt, for sprinkling

FOR THE FROSTING

170g (6oz/¾ cup) cream cheese, at room temperature

397g (14oz) can dulce de leche

240ml (8½fl oz/1 cup) double (heavy) cream, chilled

Preheat the oven to 180°C (160°C Fan) 350°F, Gas Mark 4. Lightly grease your 23 x 33cm (9 x 13in) baking tin and line it with a strip of parchment paper that overhangs the long sides, securing it in place with two metal clips.

Place the flour, baking powder, salt and sugars in a large bowl and whisk to combine. Add the butter, eggs, vanilla, espresso and sour cream and mix until a smooth batter forms. Pour it into the prepared tin and spread evenly.

Bake for about 35–40 minutes, or until the cake springs back to a light touch. Set aside to cool in the tin for 15 minutes before using the parchment paper to lift the cake onto a wire rack to cool completely.

For the frosting, place the cream cheese and dulce de leche in a large bowl and whisk until smooth. Add the cream and whisk until the mixture holds soft peaks. Spread the frosting all over the cold cake and sprinkle with flaked sea salt just before serving.

The cake can be made a couple days in advance if stored in a sealed container, but the frosting needs to be made and served on the same day.

OLIVE OIL PISTACHIO AND LEMON SNACK CAKE

SERVES 12–15

This simple pistachio cake is made in a food processor, so it takes just minutes to prepare and the machine does all the heavy lifting for you. I like to serve it with a simple lemon and sugar glaze, and sprinkled with a few roughly chopped pistachios.

200ml (7fl oz/¾ cup + 1 tablespoon) olive oil, plus extra for greasing

140g (5oz/1 cup) shelled pistachios, plus a few extra for decoration

65g (2½oz/⅔ cup) ground almonds

65g (2½oz/½ cup) gluten-free plain (all-purpose) flour

1 teaspoon baking powder

1 teaspoon fine sea salt

200g (7oz/1 cup) caster (superfine) sugar

4 large eggs

Zest of 1 lemon

FOR THE GLAZE

200g (7oz/1⅔ cups) icing (powdered) sugar

2–3 tablespoons lemon juice

Pinch of fine sea salt

Preheat the oven to 180°C (160°C Fan) 350°F, Gas Mark 4. Lightly grease your 23 x 33cm (9 x 13in) baking tin and line with a strip of parchment paper that overhangs the long sides, securing it in place with metal clips.

Place the pistachios in the bowl of a food processor fitted with the blade attachment and pulse until they are finely ground. Tip into a large bowl along with the ground almonds, flour, baking powder and salt and mix together.

Put the sugar, eggs and lemon zest in the processor bowl and process for about 1 minute. With the machine still running, slowly pour in the oil. Once fully combined, add the mixed dry ingredients and process for a second or two until evenly incorporated. Pour the batter into the prepared tin and spread evenly.

Bake for 35–40 minutes, or until lightly browned and the cake is set in the middle. Set aside to cool completely in the tin before using the parchment paper to lift it out.

For the glaze, mix the icing sugar, lemon juice and salt in a bowl until you have a thick but pourable paste. Pour it over the cake, allowing it to drip down the sides. Sprinkle with a few extra chopped pistachios to decorate.

If stored in a sealed container, the cake should keep for 3–4 days.

BANOFFEE POKE CAKE

SERVES 12–15

Banana, caramel and custard – what's not to like? As ever with all in one cakes, it's essential that the fat is very soft or it will form lumps, so leave the butter out of the refrigerator until it's good and ready. The baked cake is poked all over with the handle of a wooden spoon and these holes are filled with custard and topped with dulce de leche. The whole creation is then covered with sliced bananas and whipped cream. It's a bit messy but absolutely delicious.

170g (6oz/1½ sticks) very soft unsalted butter, plus extra for greasing

320g (11¼oz/2⅓ cups) gluten-free plain (all-purpose] flour

3½ teaspoons baking powder

½ teaspoon fine sea salt

350g (12oz/1¾ cups) caster (superfine) sugar

3 large eggs

2 teaspoons vanilla extract

195ml (6¾fl oz/¾ cup + 1 tablespoon) natural yogurt

FOR THE FILLING

240ml (8½fl oz/1 cup) thick custard, shop-bought or homemade

120ml (4fl oz/½ cup) dulce de leche

TO SERVE

4 large bananas, peeled and sliced

600ml (20fl oz/2¼ cups) double (heavy) cream

1 teaspoon vanilla bean paste

dried banana slices (optional)

Preheat the oven to 180°C (160°C Fan) 350°F, Gas Mark 4. Lightly grease your 23 x 33cm (9 x 13in) baking tin and line with a strip of parchment paper that overhangs the long sides, securing it in place with metal clips.

Put the flour, baking powder, salt and sugar in a large bowl and mix briefly to combine. Add the butter, eggs, vanilla extract and yogurt and beat with an electric mixer or wooden spoon until a smooth batter forms. Pour the batter into the prepared tin and spread evenly.

Bake for about 35 minutes, or until a skewer inserted in the middle comes out clean and the cake is just starting to pull away from the sides of the tin. Set aside to cool completely in the tin.

Once cool, use the handle of a wooden spoon to poke holes all over the top of the cake, poking about two thirds of the way through. Pour the custard onto the cake and use an offset spatula or the back of a spoon to spread it out and fill the holes. Beat the dulce de leche until loosened, then drizzle it over the cake.

To serve, arrange the sliced banana on top of the cake. Place the cream and vanilla bean paste in a bowl and whip into soft peaks, then spread over the sliced fresh banana and the dried banana slices, if using.

This cake can be made a couple days in advance, but the assembly is best done on the day it is to be eaten.

CHOCOLATE CHUNK PEANUT BUTTER SNACK CAKE

SERVES 12–15

A snack cake, devoid of fancy frostings or other extravagant adornments, is by definition one that you can happily nibble on at any point in the day. But for me the real sign of an excellent snack cake is one that magically seems to shrink over the course of a day because everyone in the house keeps going back for just a little bit more, sneaking bites they think no one will notice. This peanut butter cake is one of those recipes, as simple as it gets, but the sweet and salty nature makes it hard to resist.

65g (2½oz/4½ tablespoons) unsalted butter, melted and cooled, plus extra for greasing

265g (9½oz/2⅛ cups) plain (all-purpose) flour

220g (8oz/1 cup) light brown sugar

¾ teaspoon baking powder

1¼ teaspoons bicarbonate of soda (baking soda)

½ teaspoon fine sea salt

125g (4½oz/½ cup) smooth peanut butter, at room temperature

2 large eggs

240ml (8½fl oz/1 cup) buttermilk

100g (3½oz) milk chocolate, roughly chopped

50g (1¾oz/⅓ cup) salted peanuts, roughly chopped

Preheat the oven to 180°C (160°C Fan) 350°F, Gas Mark 4. Lightly grease your 23 x 33cm (9 x 13in) baking tin and line it with a strip of parchment paper that overhangs the long sides, securing it in place with metal clips.

Sift the flour, sugar, baking powder, bicarbonate of soda and salt into a large bowl. (Often a good whisking rather sifting will suffice, but brown sugar tends to clump, so sifting is worthwhile here.) Add the melted butter, peanut butter, eggs and buttermilk and beat with an electric mixer or wooden spoon to form a smooth batter. If using the latter, gently warming the peanut butter first can help to make the beating easier.

Pour the batter into the prepared tin and spread evenly. Scatter over the chocolate and peanuts, then bake for about 25 minutes, or until a skewer inserted into in the middle of the cake comes out clean. The cake should also be pulling slightly away from the sides of the tin.

Leave to cool in the tin for 15 minutes before using the parchment paper to transfer the cake to a wire rack to cool completely.

If stored in a sealed container, this will keep for 2–3 days.

GINGERBREAD CAKE WITH FENNEL-ROASTED PEACHES

SERVES 12

A family favourite, this recipe originates from Nanna, my maternal grandmother. I've made some tweaks to veganize it, but you'd hardly guess, as it retains all the flavour and texture of the original. If you want to make a taller cake, use the same mixture but place it in a deep square baking tin, 20 x 20cm (8 x 8in), and bake for 35–40 minutes.

160ml (5½fl oz/⅔ cup) neutral-tasting oil, plus extra for greasing

340g (11¾oz/2¾ cups) plain (all-purpose) flour

3 teaspoons ground ginger

1 teaspoon ground cinnamon

1 teaspoon mixed spice (pumpkin spice)

1 teaspoon bicarbonate of soda (baking soda)

½ teaspoon fine sea salt

110g (3¾oz/½ cup) light brown sugar

340g (11¾oz/1 cup) golden syrup or corn syrup

210ml (7½fl oz/¾ cup + 2 tablespoons) soya milk

2 vegan eggs

Whipped coconut cream, to serve

FOR THE FENNEL-ROASTED PEACHES

600g (1lb 5oz) peaches, pitted and sliced

3 tablespoons light brown sugar

1 teaspoon fennel seeds

30g (1oz/2 tablespoons) vegan butter

Juice of 1 lemon

Pinch of salt

Preheat the oven to 180°C (160°C Fan) 350°F, Gas Mark 4. Lightly grease your 23 x 33cm (9 x 13in) baking tin and line with a strip of parchment paper that overhangs the long sides, securing it in place with metal clips.

Place the flour, spices, bicarbonate of soda and salt in a large bowl and whisk together.

Put the oil, sugar, syrup and soya milk in a medium saucepan and warm over a gentle heat until the sugar has dissolved. Remove from the heat and slowly pour in the vegan eggs, whisking constantly to prevent them from going lumpy. Add this liquid to the flour mixture and whisk until smooth. Pour the batter into the prepared tin and spread evenly.

Bake for 20–25 minutes, or until the cake springs back to a light touch. Leave to cool in the tin for 20 minutes before using the parchment paper to lift the cake onto a wire rack to cool completely.

Increase the oven temperature to 200°C (180°C Fan) 400°F, Gas Mark 6. Wash and dry the empty baking tin, then add all the peach ingredients and stir to combine. Bake for 10–12 minutes, or until the fruit has softened but not broken down.

Serve slices of the cake with the peaches and a little whipped coconut cream.

If stored in a sealed container, this cake keeps incredibly well, for at least 5 days.

DEVIL'S FOOD SHEET CAKE

SERVES 12–15

Making a vegan chocolate sheet cake was an interesting challenge that involved testing all manner of dairy substitutions and egg replacements. In the end, the simplest method was the best. The butter was replaced by oil, the animal dairy by soy, and the eggs? A little bit of vinegar was all that was needed to give this cake a lift. The result is a moist and fudgy cake, perfect whether you're vegan or just in need of a great chocolate treat.

120ml (4fl oz/½ cup) neutral-tasting oil, e.g. sunflower, plus extra for greasing

250g (9oz/2 cups) plain (all-purpose) flour

75g (2¾oz/¾ cup + 2 tablespoons) cocoa powder

1 teaspoon baking powder

2 teaspoons bicarbonate of soda (baking soda)

½ teaspoon fine sea salt

300g (10½oz/1⅓ cups + 1 teaspoon) light brown sugar

240ml (8½fl oz/1 cup) dairy-free milk

240ml (8½fl oz/1 cup) hot black coffee

2 teaspoons cider vinegar

FOR THE CHOCOLATE GANACHE

125g (4½oz/½ cup + 1 tablespoon) light brown sugar

1 tablespoon cocoa powder

1 teaspoon instant espresso powder

½ teaspoon fine sea salt

400ml (14fl oz) can coconut cream, chilled

75g (2¾oz/⅓ cup) vegan butter

2 tablespoons golden syrup or brown rice syrup

325g (11½oz) dark chocolate (60% cocoa solids), finely chopped

Preheat the oven to 180°C (160°C Fan) 350°F, Gas Mark 4. Lightly grease your 23 x 33cm (9 x 13in) baking tin and line with a strip of parchment paper that overhangs the long sides, securing it in place with metal clips.

Sift the flour, cocoa powder, baking powder, bicarbonate of soda, salt and sugar into a large bowl. Make a well in the middle and pour in the remaining ingredients. Whisk together until a smooth, thin batter forms.

Pour the batter into the prepared tin and bake for about 30 minutes, or until a skewer inserted in the middle comes out clean. Set aside to cool completely in the tin.

For the ganache, put the sugar in a saucepan with the cocoa powder, espresso powder and salt and whisk together. Pour the coconut water into a jug and reserve for another recipe. Add the remaining coconut cream to the espresso mixture and whisk to form a smooth paste. Add the vegan butter and golden syrup, then place the pan over a medium heat and bring to a simmer.

Place the chocolate in a large bowl and pour the cream mixture over it. Allow to sit for a couple of minutes before stirring together to form a smooth ganache. Refrigerate until chilled but still spreadable, around 1–1½ hours, then whip until light and fluffy. If overwhipped, this mixture can become too thick and firm, so whip just until thickened and spreadable, like soft peak whipped cream.

Spread the whipped ganache over the cake and serve.

If stored in a sealed container, the cake will keep for 3–4 days, but the frosting is best made on the day of serving.

NOTE For a layer cake, divide the mixture between two round, deep baking tins, 20cm (8in) wide. Bake for 25–30 minutes.

MORE-FRUIT-THAN-CAKE CAKE

SERVES 8–10

There is no doubt that this is a cake, but the ratio of cake to fruit makes it feel more like a dessert. This isn't a cake to slice – it's a cake to be spooned into bowls while still warm and topped with a copious amount of vanilla custard or vanilla ice cream.

115g (4oz/1 stick) unsalted butter, at room temperature, plus extra for greasing

110g (3¾oz/½ cup) light brown sugar

2 large eggs

225g (8oz/1¾ cups) plain (all-purpose) flour

3 teaspoons baking powder

1 teaspoon ground cinnamon

1 teaspoon ground cardamom

½ teaspoon fine sea salt

2 tablespoons milk

6 Granny Smith apples, peeled, cored and sliced

200g (7oz) mixed berries

Demerara sugar, for sprinkling

Preheat the oven to 180ºC (160ºC Fan) 350ºF, Gas Mark 4. Lightly grease your 23 x 33cm (9 x 13in) baking tin and line the base with parchment paper.

Place the butter and light brown sugar in a large bowl and beat together for about 5 minutes, until light and fluffy. Beat in the eggs one at a time, beating well between each addition. Add the flour, baking powder, spices and salt and mix together to form a batter, stirring though the milk to loosen slightly. Add the fruit and fold in briefly, just to combine.

Pour the batter into the prepared tin and spread evenly, then sprinkle liberally with demerara sugar.

Bake for about 30 minutes, or until the cake springs back to a light touch. There is so much fruit in this cake that it can be a tricky to judge when it's fully baked. Testing with a skewer is not totally reliable, so look for the cake starting to pull away from the sides of the tin.

Serve straight from the tin while still warm, with lashings of custard or vanilla ice cream.

The cake is best eaten on the day it is made.

LEMON AND LIME COURGETTE CAKE

SERVES 12

Courgette (zucchini) is the neglected member of the vegetable cake family and I'm not sure why. It works just as well as carrots, pumpkin and beetroot (beet), and is perhaps more versatile because it has less flavour than its friends and is a great blank canvas for combining with other ingredients. If you've ever made a carrot cake, this recipe will feel familiar, but do remember to remove as much moisture as possible from the courgette or your cake could end up mushy or heavy.

75ml (2¾fl oz/5 tablespoons) olive oil, plus extra for greasing

200g (7oz) courgette (zucchini), grated

275g (10oz/1¼ cups + 2 tablespoons) caster (superfine) sugar

Zest of 2 limes

Zest of 1 lemon

3 vegan eggs made with a mixture of lemon and lime juice (see page 14)

270ml (9¾fl oz/1⅛ cups) soya or other plant-based milk yogurt

250g (9oz/2 cups) plain (all-purpose) flour

1 teaspoon baking powder

½ teaspoon bicarbonate of soda (baking soda)

½ teaspoon fine sea salt

FOR THE GLAZE

30ml (1fl oz/2 tablespoons) lemon or lime juice, or a mixture of the two

120g (4¼oz/1 cup) icing (powdered) sugar

Preheat the oven to 180°C (160°C Fan) 350°F, Gas Mark 4. Lightly grease your 23 x 33cm (9 x 13in) baking tin and line with a strip of parchment paper that overhangs the long sides, securing it in place with metal clips.

First remove excess moisture from the grated courgette: place it on a clean tea towel (kitchen towel), wrap it up tightly, then squeeze as hard as you can to get rid of its moisture content.

Put the sugar and all but 2 teaspoons of the citrus zest in a large bowl and rub together with your fingers until the sugar resembles wet sand. (The rubbing helps to bring out the oils in the zest, increasing the flavour.) Add the olive oil, vegan eggs and soya yogurt and whisk together until smooth. Now add the courgette and stir to combine. Stir in the flour, baking powder, bicarbonate of soda and salt until a smooth batter forms. Pour the batter into the prepared tin and spread evenly.

Bake for 30–35 minutes, or until lightly browned and the cake springs back to a light touch. Remove from the oven and allow to cool fully before removing from the tin.

For the glaze, mix the citrus juice with the icing sugar until smooth. Drizzle over the cold cake and finish by sprinkling with the reserved citrus zest.

Stored in a sealed container, this cake will keep for 3–4 days.

VICTORIA SHEET CAKE

SERVES 12–15

This is the classic British Victoria sponge given the sheet cake treatment. For many Brits reading this, a Victoria sponge would have been the first cake they learned to make, and perhaps also the first cake they ever ate. While it's certainly an old recipe, it remains incredibly popular, and rightly so.

225g (8oz/2 sticks) very soft unsalted butter, plus extra for greasing

225g (8oz/1¾ cups + 2 teaspoons) plain (all-purpose) flour

3½ teaspoons baking powder

½ teaspoon fine sea salt

225g (8oz/1⅛ cups) caster (superfine) sugar

4 large eggs, lightly beaten

FOR THE TOPPING

200g (7oz/½ cup + 2 tablespoons) raspberry jam

600ml (20fl oz/2½ cups) double (heavy) cream

1 teaspoon vanilla bean paste

Preheat the oven to 180°C (160°C Fan) 350°F, Gas Mark 4. Lightly grease your 23 x 33cm (9 x 13in) baking tin and line with a strip of parchment paper that overhangs the long sides, securing it in place with metal clips.

Put the flour, baking powder, salt and sugar in a large bowl and whisk to combine. Add the butter and eggs and mix together until a smooth batter forms. Pour the batter into the prepared tin and spread evenly.

Bake for 25–30 minutes, or until the cake is golden and coming away from the sides of the tin. Leave to cool in the tin for about 20 minutes before using the parchment paper to lift the cake onto a wire rack to cool completely.

Spread the jam over the cake. Lightly whisk the cream and vanilla together into soft peaks, then spread over the jam.

This cake is best served on the day it is made, but it can be made the day before if needed. If stored in a sealed container, add the topping just before serving.

PUMPKIN SHEET CAKE WITH MAPLE BUTTER GLAZE

SERVES 10–12

When anything is labelled as 'pumpkin' I am inevitably disappointed. Not because the flavour isn't good, but because these things are sometimes made without actual pumpkin, just pumpkin spice, and it feels like I am being cheated out of something. This pumpkin sheet cake is made with both pumpkin purée and plenty of spices to give a tender bake reminiscent of carrot cake, but full of autumnal flavour. The topping is a simple maple butter glaze, but if you want to give a further boost of flavour, you could brown the butter first (see page 28).

180ml (6¼fl oz/¾ cup) olive oil, plus extra for greasing

250g (9oz/2 cups) plain (all-purpose) flour

2½ teaspoons baking powder

1 teaspoon bicarbonate of soda (baking soda)

½ teaspoon fine sea salt

2 teaspoons ground cinnamon

½ teaspoon ground allspice

½ teaspoon ground cardamom

½ teaspoon ground nutmeg

300g (10½oz/1⅓ cups + 1 teaspoon) light brown sugar

3 large eggs

425g (15oz) can pumpkin purée

Toasted pumpkin seeds, for sprinkling

FOR THE GLAZE

30g (1oz/2 tablespoons) soft unsalted butter

60ml (2¼fl oz/¼ cup) maple syrup

120g (4¼oz/1 cup) icing (powdered) sugar

Pinch of salt

Splash of milk

Preheat the oven to 180°C (160°C Fan) 350°F, Gas Mark 4. Lightly grease the baking tin and line with a strip of parchment paper that overhangs the long sides, securing it in place with metal clips.

Sift the flour, baking powder, bicarbonate of soda, salt, spices and sugar into a large bowl, then whisk to combine. Make a well in the centre and add the eggs, pumpkin purée and oil. Whisk together until a smooth batter forms. Pour into the prepared tin and spread evenly.

Bake for 30–35 minutes, or until a skewer inserted into the middle of the cake comes out clean. Transfer the tin to a wire rack to cool completely. Leave to cool in the tin for 15 minutes before using the parchment paper to lift the cake onto a wire rack to cool completely.

Combine all the glaze ingredients, except the milk, in a bowl and beat until smooth. Add just enough milk to make a pourable consistency. Pour the glaze over the cooled cake and tease it to the edges so it drips down the sides. Top with a generous sprinkling of lightly toasted pumpkin seeds.

If stored in a sealed container, this cake will keep for about 3 days.

BROWN SUGAR BUTTERSCOTCH CAKE

SERVES 12–15

Here is proof that brown food is best. This moist brown sugar sheet cake topped with a vanilla-rich buttercream and a super-simple butterscotch sauce is the sort of cake I want someone to make me for my birthday. The sauce is very easy to make, and provides more than you'll need for this cake, so store it in the refrigerator for another occasion. It keeps well but becomes thick and opaque, so rewarm it gently to make it usable again.

210ml (7½fl oz/¾ cup + 2 tablespoons) vegetable oil, plus extra for greasing

420g (15oz/3⅓ cups) cups plain (all-purpose) flour

345g (11¾oz/1½ cups + 1 tablespoon) light brown sugar

4 teaspoons baking powder

1 teaspoon salt

3 vegan eggs

350ml (12fl oz/1⅓ cups + 2 tablespoons) soya milk

Cacao nibs, for sprinkling

FOR THE BUTTERSCOTCH SAUCE

120g (4¼oz/½ cup + 2 teaspoons) light brown sugar

80g (2¾oz/⅓ cup) vegan butter

1 teaspoon vanilla bean paste

½ teaspoon fine sea salt

120ml (4fl oz/½ cup) coconut cream

FOR THE VANILLA BUTTERCREAM

170g (6oz/1½ sticks) vegan butter

350g (12oz/scant 3 cups) icing (powdered) sugar

2 teaspoons vanilla bean paste

¼ teaspoon fine sea salt

2 tablespoons non-dairy milk

For the butterscotch sauce, place the sugar, vegan butter, vanilla and salt in a medium saucepan and heat until the butter has melted and everything is bubbling. Heat for another 2–3 minutes, then pour in the coconut cream and heat for a further 2 minutes, until reduced to a slightly syrupy consistency. Pour into a jug and set aside to cool; it should have a pourable caramel consistency. The sauce can be refrigerated until needed, but might need to be warmed gently to make it pourable again.

Preheat the oven to 180°C (160°C Fan) 350°F, Gas Mark 4. Lightly grease your 23 x 33cm (9 x 13in) baking tin and line with a strip of parchment paper that overhangs the long sides, securing it in place with metal clips.

For the cake, put the flour, sugar, baking powder and salt in a large bowl and whisk to combine. Add the vegan eggs, oil and soya milk and whisk to form a smooth batter. Pour the batter into the prepared tin and spread evenly.

Bake for 35–40 minutes, or until a skewer inserted in the middle of the cake comes out clean. Leave to cool in the tin for 20 minutes before using the parchment paper to lift the cake onto a wire rack to cool completely.

For the buttercream, put the vegan butter into a large bowl and beat with an electric mixer until light and creamy. Add the icing sugar a few spoonfuls at a time, beating well between each addition. Once all the sugar has been incorporated, add the vanilla and salt and beat on a high speed for about 5 minutes, or until light and fluffy. Add the non-dairy milk and beat to combine.

To assemble the cake, spread it with the buttercream, then drizzle over some butterscotch sauce, gently swirling it into the buttercream. Sprinkle over the cacao nibs.

If stored in a sealed container, this will keep for 2–3 days.

BARS & COOKIES

SALTED CHOCOLATE AND CARAMEL REVEL BARS

MAKES 12–15

I was introduced to revel bars, a classic recipe from the American Midwest, by my food writer friend Shauna Sever. In her brilliant book *Midwest Made* she shares a recipe for espresso and chocolate revel bars, and this recipe is a spin on that wonderful idea. Here I've filled the slightly chewy oatmeal dough with chocolate and caramel. These bars are best made when you know you'll have friends to serve them to, otherwise you might walk into the kitchen in a sugar-induced haze and wonder who on earth ate them all. Reader, it was you!

275g (10oz/2 cups) gluten-free plain (all-purpose) flour

½ teaspoon xanthan gum (omit if your flour blend already includes it)

1 teaspoon bicarbonate of soda (baking soda)

1 teaspoon fine sea salt

250g (9oz/3⅛ cups) rolled oats

330g (11½oz/1½ cups) light brown sugar

200g (7oz/1¾ sticks) unsalted butter, melted and cooled, plus extra for greasing

2 large eggs

1 teaspoon vanilla extract

FOR THE FILLING

90ml (3¼fl oz/⅓ cup + 2 teaspoons) double (heavy) cream

35g (1¼oz/2½ tablespoons) light brown sugar

125g (4½oz) dark chocolate (60–70% cocoa solids), finely chopped

100g (3½oz) chewy caramels (I use Werther's brand)

First up, we need to make the filling so it has time to thicken. Bring the cream and sugar to a simmer in a small saucepan. Place the chocolate in a heatproof bowl, pour the cream mixture over it and leave for a minute or two before stirring to make a smooth ganache. Set aside for about an hour until cooled and slightly thickened.

Preheat the oven to 180ºC (160ºC Fan) 350ºF, Gas Mark 4. Lightly grease your 23 x 33cm (9 x 13in) baking tin and line with a strip of parchment paper that overhangs the long sides, securing it in place with metal clips.

Place the flour, xanthan gum (if using), bicarbonate of soda, salt, oats and sugar in a large bowl and stir to combine. Make a well in the middle, add the melted butter, eggs and vanilla and stir until a soft dough forms. Spoon about two-thirds of the dough into the prepared tin and spread evenly, using the back of the spoon or a small offset spatula. If you find the spreading difficult, you can use wet hands to press it into place, the water helping to prevent the dough sticking too much.

Drizzle thick ribbons of the chocolate ganache over the dough. Cut the caramels into small nuggets and scatter them over the top. Dollop spoonfuls of the remaining dough randomly over the surface.

Bake for 30–35 minutes, or until lightly browned. Leave to cool completely in the tin.

Use the parchment paper to carefully lift the bars from the tin, then use a sharp knife to cut into pieces.

Stored in a sealed container, these will keep for 3–4 days.

TAHINI BROWNIES

MAKES 12–15

I have tested numerous recipes for vegan brownies, but I promise you that this is the one, the ultimate vegan brownie. My early tests were either so fudgy it was like eating, well, fudge, or oddly gritty and separated. In the end the style of recipe that worked best was a cocoa-based brownie. It reacted very well to vegan ingredients, giving a fabulously dense and slightly chewy texture and an intense chocolate flavour. To complement that I have included a super-simple tahini glaze, the nuttiness of the tahini being a perfect partner for the chocolate.

300g (10½oz/1⅓ cups) vegan butter, plus extra for greasing

220g (8oz/1 cup) light brown sugar

150g (5½oz/¾ cup) caster (superfine) sugar

150g (5½oz/1¾ cups) cocoa powder

½ teaspoon fine sea salt

1 teaspoon vanilla extract

4 vegan eggs

125g (4½oz/1 cup) plain (all-purpose) flour

170g (6oz) dark chocolate, roughly chopped

Sesame seeds, for sprinkling

FOR THE GLAZE

2 tablespoons tahini

1 tablespoon maple syrup

1–2 teaspoons water

Large pinch of flaked sea salt

Preheat the oven to 180°C (160°C Fan) 350°F, Gas Mark 4. Lightly grease your 23 x 33cm (9 x 13in) baking tin and line with a strip of parchment paper that overhangs the long sides, securing it in place with metal clips.

Place the butter, sugars, cocoa powder and salt in a large heatproof bowl and set over a pan of simmering water. Heat, stirring occasionally, until everything is fully melted. The mixture will look grainy or even like the fat is separating, but that's absolutely fine. Remove the bowl from the heat and stir in the vanilla. Set aside for the moment.

Add the vegan eggs to the batter and whisk until smooth. Initially, you might find that the two mixtures don't want to combine, but they will eventually emulsify into a smooth, shiny batter. Add the flour and chocolate and mix until the flour disappears. Pour the batter into the prepared tin and spread evenly.

Bake for 30 minutes, or until a skewer inserted in the middle comes out with moist crumbs. Set aside to cool completely, then use the parchment paper to lift carefully from the tin.

For the glaze, combine the tahini, maple syrup, water and salt in a bowl and mix to a smooth, pourable consistency. Drizzle all over the brownies and sprinkle with sesame seeds. Cut into pieces and serve.

Stored in a sealed container, these brownies will keep for 3–4 days.

OATMEAL GINGER SLICE

MAKES 16–24

A slice, for the uninitiated, is the Australian and New Zealand equivalent of a British traybake, a super-simple recipe baked in a rectangular tin. The range of Antipodean slices is seemingly never-ending, from the traditional and classic to the modern and inventive. This recipe is inspired by a classic New Zealand slice that is traditionally made with a shortbread-style base, but my friend Erin Clarkson, a NZ food blogger, makes them with an oatmeal-style base, and now I make them no other way. The chewy base is topped with a sweet but fiery ginger icing, so I serve the slice in smaller pieces than other bars. The flavours make them hard to resist, so make these when you have a crowd to feed.

160g (5¾oz/⅔ cup + 2 teaspoons) unsalted butter, plus extra for greasing

165g (5¾oz/1½ cups) plain (all-purpose) flour

220g (8oz/2¾ cups) rolled oats

4 tablespoons golden syrup or clear honey

180g (6¼oz/¾ cup + 1 tablespoon) light brown sugar

1 teaspoon bicarbonate of soda (baking soda)

FOR THE GINGER ICING

150g (5½oz/1⅓ sticks) unsalted butter

4 tablespoons golden syrup or clear honey

2 tablespoons ground ginger

240g (8½oz/2 cups) icing (powdered) sugar

1 teaspoon vanilla bean paste

Pinch of fine sea salt

Preheat the oven to 180°C (160°C Fan) 350°F, Gas Mark 4. Lightly grease your 23 x 33cm (9 x 13in) baking tin and line with a strip of parchment paper that overhangs the long sides, securing it in place with metal clips.

For the base, combine the flour and oats in a bowl. Put the butter, golden syrup and sugar into a saucepan and heat until melted and smooth. Remove from the heat, add the bicarbonate of soda and mix briefly to combine. Pour this mixture into the dry ingredients and mix until thoroughly combined.

Pour the mixture into the prepared tin and spread evenly. This is best done with a small offset spatula or the back of a metal spoon, as the layer is thin.

Bake for 20–25 minutes, until the base is golden, a little darker around the edges and a touch paler in the centre. Set aside for the moment.

For the icing, put all the ingredients into a saucepan, place over a medium heat and cook, stirring constantly, until the mixture is fully melted and smooth. Pour it over the still-hot base and spread evenly. Set aside at room temperature until the icing has set.

Use the parchment paper to carefully lift the slice from the tin, then use a sharp knife to cut into small pieces.

Stored in a sealed container, these slices will keep for about 3–4 days.

NOTE To make a vegan version, simply replace the butter with a non-dairy alternative, and if you can't find golden syrup, use brown rice syrup instead.

BLUEBERRY SOUR CREAM BARS

MAKES 16

I love these bars because they somehow seem sophisticated, yet are incredibly quick and easy to put together as they are made in a food processor. The simple oatmeal cookie part is pleasingly soft and tender, and includes just a touch of cinnamon, not to give the recipe any real spicing but to enhance the oat flavour. The filling is a little like cheesecake, but lighter and fresher, making it a nice balance to the sweet oatmeal cookie.

250g (9oz/2 cups) plain (all-purpose) flour

200g (7oz/2½ cups) rolled oats

220g (8oz/1 cup) light brown sugar

½ teaspoon ground cinnamon

½ teaspoon fine sea salt

½ teaspoon bicarbonate of soda (baking soda)

225g (8oz/2 sticks) unsalted butter, chilled and diced, plus extra for greasing

2 large egg yolks

FOR THE FILLING

480ml (17fl oz/2 cups) sour cream

150g (5½oz/¾ cup) caster (superfine) sugar

4 tablespoons cornflour (cornstarch)

2 large eggs

1 teaspoon vanilla bean paste

300g (10½oz) blueberries

Preheat the oven to 180°C (160°C Fan) 350°F, Gas Mark 4. Lightly grease your 23 x 33cm (9 x 13in) baking tin and line it with a large single sheet of parchment paper that fully covers both base and sides.

Place the flour, oats, sugar, cinnamon, salt and bicarbonate of soda in the bowl of a food processor fitted with the blade attachment and pulse for about 10 seconds, or until evenly mixed and the oats have slightly broken down. Add the butter and process until the mixture looks like breadcrumbs. Add the egg yolks and pulse briefly, just until the dough starts to clump together.

Tip half the mixture into the prepared tin and press into an even layer. Place the remainder in the refrigerator.

Bake the base for about 20 minutes, or until pale golden. Set aside for the moment.

For the filling, simply whisk the sour cream, sugar, cornflour, eggs and vanilla together in a bowl, then stir in the blueberries. Pour the filling onto the base and spread evenly. Scatter over the remaining dough mixture and bake for 35–40 minutes, or until the filling is set and the topping is browned. Allow to cool to room temperature before transferring to the refrigerator for a few hours to cool completely.

Use the parchment paper to carefully lift the bars from the tin, then use a sharp knife to cut into pieces, wiping off the blade between cuts to get neat slices.

If refrigerated, these bars will keep for 3–4 days, but will slowly soften, becoming more cake-like in texture.

SAMOA BARS

MAKES 15

In the UK we're not lucky enough to have access to American Girl Scout cookies, and that's a big problem, at least for me. My yearly cravings for thin mint and Samoa cookies remains unfulfilled. Thankfully, both are relatively easy to replicate at home. These simple bars are my vegan take on the classic Samoa cookie, made with shortbread, coconut milk caramel, lots of toasted coconut and generous drizzles of dark chocolate.

145g (5¼oz/⅔ cup) unrefined coconut oil, melted, plus extra for greasing

350g (12oz/2¾ cups) plain (all-purpose) flour

40g (1½oz/2 tablespoons) icing (powdered) sugar

¼ teaspoon fine sea salt

75ml (2¾fl oz/5 tablespoons) maple syrup

70g (2½oz) dark chocolate, melted, for decorating

FOR THE COCONUT CARAMEL

150g (5½oz/2 cups) desiccated coconut

45ml (1¾fl oz/3 tablespoons) unrefined coconut oil

320g (11¼oz) can condensed coconut milk

2 tablespoons golden syrup or maple syrup

55g (2oz/¼ cup) light brown sugar

Lightly grease your 23 x 33cm (9 x 13in) baking tin and line with a large single sheet of parchment paper that fully covers both base and sides.

Place the flour, icing sugar and salt in a large bowl. Put the coconut oil and maple syrup in a small saucepan and heat until the oil has fully melted. Make a well in the bowl of dry ingredients and pour in the oil mixture. Stir with a spatula or wooden spoon until a dough forms. Tip the mixture into the prepared tin and press into a flat, even layer. Dock the surface with a fork, then refrigerate for 30 minutes, or until the base is firm.

Preheat the oven to 180°C (160°C Fan) 350°F, Gas Mark 4. Place the coconut in a dry frying pan and toast over a medium heat, stirring occasionally, until golden. Tip into a bowl and set aside for the moment.

Once the chilled base is firm, bake for 25–30 minutes, or until golden and the edges are a touch darker. Set aside.

For the caramel, place the coconut oil, condensed coconut milk, golden syrup and sugar in a saucepan and place over a medium heat, stirring continuously until the colour deepens a little and the mixture slightly thickens. (If you've ever made a traditional [non-vegan] condensed milk caramel, it's worth noting that this version won't thicken or darken in quite the same way.) If you want to guarantee it is cooked enough, heat the caramel until it reaches 112°C (234°F) on an instant-read or sugar thermometer.

Remove the pan from the heat and stir in the toasted coconut, then immediately spread the mixture over the shortbread. Set aside to cool at room temperature.

To finish, use the parchment paper to carefully lift the bars from the tin, then drizzle over the melted chocolate, using a spoon or a piping bag. Use a sharp knife to cut the shortbread into pieces.

Stored in a sealed container, these will keep for 4 days.

CHOCOLATE CHIP PECAN PIE BARS

MAKES 12

These pecan pie-inspired bars are for people who can't muster the energy to make a full-blown pie, pastry and all. The base is a quick shortbread dough that is baked and then topped with a pecan pie-style custard, the only difference being that, in a throwback to vintage American baking, I have replaced some of the pecans with oats.

350g (12oz/2¾ cups) plain (all-purpose) flour

200g (7oz/1 cup) caster (superfine) sugar

¼ teaspoon fine sea salt

225g (8oz/2 sticks) unsalted butter, melted and cooled

85g (3oz/½ cup) mini chocolate chips

FOR THE TOPPING

300g (10½oz/¾ cup + 2 tablespoons) golden syrup or corn syrup

4 large eggs

100g (3½oz/⅓ cup + 2 tablespoons) light brown sugar

¼ teaspoon fine sea salt

3 tablespoons dark spiced rum or other dark liquor, e.g. whisky (optional)

1 teaspoon ground cinnamon

1 teaspoon vanilla extract

50g (1¾oz/⅔ cup) rolled oats

150g (5½oz/1¼ cups) roughly chopped pecans

Lightly grease your 23 x 33cm (9 x 13in) baking tin and line with a large single sheet of parchment paper that fully covers both base and sides.

Place the flour, sugar and salt in a large bowl and stir to combine. Make a well in the middle, then pour in the melted butter and mix with a butter knife until a dough just starts to form. Add the chocolate chips and stir briefly to distribute.

Scrape the mixture into the prepared tin and press into an even layer. Refrigerate for 30 minutes, or until firm.

Preheat the oven to 180ºC (160ºC Fan) 350ºF, Gas Mark 4. Dock the chilled biscuit base with a fork and bake for about 35 minutes, or until golden brown. Set aside, but keep the oven on while you prepare the topping.

Put the golden syrup, eggs, sugar, salt, rum (if using), cinnamon and vanilla into a large bowl and whisk together until smooth. Add the oats and pecans and whisk to combine. Pour the filling onto the biscuit base and spread around a little to cover evenly.

Bake for about 30 minutes, or until the topping is set. Set aside to cool completely in the tin.

Use the parchment paper to carefully lift out the bars, then use a sharp knife to cut into pieces.

If stored in a sealed container, the bars will keep for 3–4 days, but the base will soften over time.

NOTE Once the bars have cooled, refrigerating them for 30 minutes or so can make it easier to lift them from the tin and also help with cutting neat squares.

LIME MELTING MOMENT BARS

MAKES 12

These incredibly easy cookie bars use cornflour (cornstarch) to make a wonderfully tender shortbread-style bar that is topped with a lime curd: impressive yet simple. While I would always encourage you to use homemade lime curd for optimal flavour, I will look the other way if you want to use a shop-bought version.

225g (8oz/2 sticks) unsalted butter, plus extra for greasing, at room temperature

90g (3¼oz/¾ cup) icing (powdered) sugar, plus extra for dusting

1 teaspoon vanilla extract

250g (9oz/2 cups) plain (all-purpose) flour

40g (1½oz/⅓ cup) cornflour (cornstarch)

½ teaspoon fine sea salt

FOR THE LIME CURD

Zest and juice of 4 limes

135g (4¾oz/⅔ cup) caster (superfine) sugar

65g (2½oz/4½ tablespoons) unsalted butter, diced

3 large eggs

Lightly grease your 23 x 33cm (9 x 13in) baking tin and line with a large single sheet of parchment paper that fully covers both base and sides.

Place the butter, sugar and vanilla in a large bowl and beat until light and creamy, about 5 minutes or so. Add the flour, cornflour and salt and mix until a soft dough forms. Scrape the dough into the prepared tin and spread evenly. Refrigerate for about an hour, until firm.

Meanwhile, place all the lime curd ingredients in a heatproof bowl set over a pan of simmering water and stir until the mixture has thickened enough to coat the back of a wooden spoon, almost like custard. If you want to ensure you have fully cooked the curd, you can test it with an instant-read or jam thermometer, which should register 75–80°C (167–176°F). Take the bowl off the heat and press a sheet of clingfilm (plastic wrap) directly on the surface of the curd. Refrigerate until needed.

Preheat the oven to 180°C (160°C Fan) 350°F, Gas Mark 4.

When the dough is firm, use the handle of a wooden spoon to make diagonal line impressions across the base of the dough. Alternatively, use your thumb to make divots all across the dough.

Bake for 15 minutes, then check how the depressions look; if they've puffed up, gently press them back into shape. Return to the oven for another 10 minutes, or until golden. Spoon or pipe the curd into the depressions and bake for a further 5 minutes or so, until the curd has set. Leave to cool for 20 minutes, then refrigerate until cold.

Use the parchment paper to carefully lift the bars from the tin, dust with a little icing sugar and then use a sharp knife to cut into pieces.

If stored in a sealed container, these bars will keep for about 3 days.

NOTE If you decide to make a smaller batch of these bars, it is still worth making a full batch of curd, as it keeps very well in the refrigerator and is great to have on hand.

EVERYTHING-BUT-THE-KITCHEN-SINK COOKIES

MAKES 12–15

Here's a recipe into which you can throw all those snack ingredients hanging about in the back of your cupboard to make a glorious mess of a cookie. I suggest below what might be included, but really you can use whatever you want or have to hand. My advice would be to keep the chocolate as stated, to add some form of dried fruit, and to include at least one crunchy, salty element – for example, raisins, peanut butter chips, chunks of toffee, oats, marshmallows, peanuts … it's a true kid-in-a-candy-store cookie.

170g (6oz/1½ sticks) unsalted butter, at room temperature, plus extra for greasing

125g (4½oz/½ cup + 2 tablespoons) caster (superfine) sugar

125g (4½oz/½ cup + 1 tablespoon) light brown sugar

2 large eggs

1 teaspoon vanilla extract

310g (10¾oz/2½ cups) plain (all-purpose) flour

¾ teaspoon bicarbonate of soda (baking soda)

¾ teaspoon baking powder

½ teaspoon fine sea salt

65g (2½oz/½ cup) dried cranberries or dried sour cherries

75g (2¾oz/⅔ cup) pecans, roughly chopped

70g (2½oz/1½ cups) salted pretzels

70g (2½oz/2 cups) salted crisps (potato chips)

170g (6oz) dark chocolate, roughly chopped

2 tablespoons finely ground coffee

Preheat the oven to 180ºC (160ºC Fan) 350ºF, Gas Mark 4. Lightly grease your 23 x 33cm (9 x 13in) baking tin and line with a strip of parchment paper so that it overhangs the long sides, securing it in place with metal clips.

Place the butter and sugars in a large bowl and beat with an electric mixer for about 5 minutes, until light and fluffy. Add the eggs one at a time, beating until each is fully combined before adding the next. Add the vanilla and beat briefly to combine.

In a separate bowl, whisk together the flour, bicarbonate of soda, baking powder and salt. Add the flour mixture to the egg mixture and mix just until combined. Add the cranberries, pecans, pretzels, crisps, chocolate and coffee, or whatever mix-ins you like, reserving a small amount for decoration. Stir until thoroughly combined.

Scrape the dough into the prepared tin and spread evenly. Sprinkle the reserved mix-ins over the surface and gently press them into the dough.

Bake for 25–30 minutes, until browned. Set aside to cool completely in the tin.

Use the parchment paper to carefully lift the bars from the tin, then use a sharp knife to cut into pieces.

Stored in a sealed container, the cookies will keep for about 3–4 days.

DREAM BARS

MAKES 12

Tender, crumbly shortbread, dark chocolate and espresso meringue? That's my sort of dream, no doubt about that. To keep this as simple as possible, I make the shortbread in a food processor, but if you don't have one, you can also make it by hand, using the same rubbing-in method as pastry. Given the lengthy whisking needed by the vegan meringue, I recommend using some form of electric whisk, as doing it by hand is nigh on impossible.

150g (5½oz/1⅓ sticks) vegan butter, diced, plus extra for greasing

235g (8½oz/1¾ cups + 2 tablespoons) plain (all-purpose) flour

75g (2¾oz/¼ cup + 2 tablespoons) caster (superfine) sugar

¾ teaspoon fine sea salt

100g (3½oz) dark chocolate, finely chopped

FOR THE MERINGUE TOPPING

400g (14oz) can chickpeas (garbanzos)

⅛ teaspoon cream of tartar

125g (4½oz/1⅛ cups) caster (superfine) sugar

1½ teaspoons instant espresso powder

½ teaspoon vanilla bean paste

Preheat the oven to 180°C (160°C Fan) 350°F, Gas Mark 4. Lightly grease your 23 x 33cm (9 x 13in) baking tin and line with large single sheet of parchment paper that fully covers both base and sides.

Place the flour, sugar and salt in the bowl of a food processor fitted with the blade attachment, and pulse briefly to combine. Add the vegan butter and process just until a dough starts to clump together. Tip the crumbly mixture into the prepared tin and spread evenly, then use your hands to compact it. Freeze for 10 minutes, until firm.

Bake for 30–35 minutes, or until golden brown. Sprinkle the chocolate over the hot shortbread, then set aside for a couple of minutes to melt. Using a palette knife, spread evenly, then set aside again.

Reduce the oven temperature to 120°C (100°C Fan) 250°F, Gas Mark ½.

For the meringue, strain the liquid from the chickpeas (this is known as aquafaba) and measure 100ml (3½fl oz/⅓ cup + 4 teaspoons) of the aquafaba into a large bowl. Add the cream of tartar and whisk with an electric mixer for 5–10 minutes, or until the meringue holds stiff peaks and doesn't slip around when the bowl is turned upside down. Very gradually add the sugar, whisking well between each addition. Once all the sugar has been incorporated, whisk until the meringue is stiff and the sugar has fully dissolved. Add the espresso powder and vanilla and whisk for a minute or so to combine.

Scrape the meringue onto the shortbread and spread evenly. Bake for about 1½ hours, until the meringue is crisp and dry. Turn off the oven but leave the tin inside it to cool down slowly.

Use the parchment paper to carefully lift the bars from the tin, then use a fine sharp knife to cut into pieces, wiping the blade clean after each cut.

Stored in a sealed container, these will keep for 2–3 days.

NOTE The leftover aquafaba from the tin of chickpeas can be refrigerated for another use and kept for up to a week after opening.

BARS & COOKIES

PBJ THUMBPRINT BARS

MAKES 12–16

Halfway between a cookie and a blondie, these PBJ (peanut butter jelly) bars are delightfully chewy and have a great flavour; salty and sweet with pockets of raspberry jam, they're the definition of moreish. I recommend using smooth commercial peanut butter, as the natural type has a negative impact on the texture of these bars.

135g (4¾oz/9½ tablespoons) unsalted butter, at room temperature, plus extra for greasing

250g (9oz/2 cups) plain (all-purpose) flour

1 teaspoon baking powder

½ teaspoon fine sea salt

150g (5½oz/¾ cup) caster (superfine) sugar

175g (6oz/⅔ cup + 2 tablespoons) light brown sugar

130g (4¾oz/½ cup) smooth peanut butter

1 teaspoon vanilla extract

2 large eggs

160g (5¾oz/½ cup) raspberry jam

75g (2¾oz/⅔ cup) salted peanuts, roughly chopped

FOR THE DRIZZLE

50g (1¾oz) white chocolate, melted

1 tablespoon smooth peanut butter, gently warmed

Preheat the oven to 180ºC (160ºC Fan) 350ºF, Gas Mark 4. Lightly grease your 23 x 33cm (9 x 13in) baking tin and line with a strip of parchment paper that overhangs the long sides, securing it in place with metal clips.

Place the flour, baking powder and salt in a large bowl and whisk together.

Place the butter, sugars and peanut butter in a separate large bowl and beat with an electric mixer for about 5 minutes, until light and fluffy. Add the vanilla and beat briefly to combine. Add the eggs one at a time, beating until each is fully incorporated before adding the next. Add the flour mixture and beat on a low speed until evenly combined.

Scrape the batter into the prepared tin and spread evenly. Using a small spoon, or the handle of a wooden spoon, make lots of little holes over the surface of the dough, then fill them with jam. Sprinkle over the chopped peanuts, trying to avoid the jam.

Bake for about 35 minutes, or until set and firm around the edges. Set aside to cool completely in the tin. Use the parchment paper to carefully lift the bars from the tin, then use a sharp knife to cut into pieces.

For the topping, mix together the white chocolate and peanut butter and drizzle over the bars, using a spoon or a piping bag.

Stored in a sealed container, these will keep for 3–4 days.

FROSTED OATMEAL CREAM BARS

MAKES 16

Some consider oatmeal cookies to be old fashioned, even a little bit boring, but I think they can be just as good as chocolate chip cookies. One of my favourite versions is called an oatmeal cream pie, which consists of two soft oatmeal cookies sandwiched with a marshmallow-like filling. This bar version tries to capture some of that magic, with a healthy dose of nostalgia for good measure. The cream filling is traditionally made with shop-bought marshmallow fluff, but since that isn't easy to find outside the US, I make a super-fluffy vanilla cream frosting instead.

150g (5½oz/1⅓ sticks) unsalted butter, melted, plus extra for greasing

250g (9oz/1 cup + 4 tablespoons) light brown sugar

1 large egg

2 large egg yolks

200g (7oz/2½ cups) rolled oats

150g (5½oz/1 cup + 3 tablespoons) plain (all-purpose) flour

¾ teaspoon bicarbonate of soda (baking soda)

1 teaspoon fine sea salt

1 teaspoon ground cinnamon

FOR THE FROSTING

100g (3½oz/7 tablespoons) unsalted butter, at room temperature

200g (7oz/1⅔ cups) icing (powdered) sugar

80ml (3fl oz/⅓ cup) double (heavy) cream

Large pinch of fine sea salt

1 teaspoon vanilla bean paste

Preheat the oven to 180ºC (160ºC Fan) 350ºF, Gas Mark 4. Lightly grease your 23 x 33cm (9 x 13in) baking tin and line with a strip of parchment paper that overhangs the long sides, securing it in place with metal clips.

Place the butter and light brown sugar in a large bowl and whisk together until combined. Add the egg and whisk thoroughly, then add the yolks and whisk again until fully combined. Add the oats, flour, bicarbonate of soda, salt and cinnamon and stir together until a uniform dough forms.

Scrape the dough into the prepared tin and spread evenly. Bake for 25–30 minutes, or until lightly browned, puffed around the edges and set in the middle. Set aside to cool completely in the tin.

For the frosting, beat the butter and icing sugar in a bowl until light and fluffy, at least 5 minutes. Add the cream, salt and vanilla, then beat briefly until smooth and combined.

Use the parchment paper to carefully lift the bars from the tin, then spread evenly with the frosting. Use a sharp knife to cut into pieces.

If stored in a sealed container and refrigerated, these bars will keep for 2–3 days.

LEMON BARS

MAKES 24 SMALL BARS

When you bake with lemon, the result should be mouth-puckeringly sharp. Lemon bars give that bite, that tingle, and thankfully they're very simple to make. My preference is for a silky smooth topping, so I put no flour in the lemon mixture, just a little cornflour to help stabilize the mix. The added benefit of this is that it makes the lemon mixture gluten-free, so I have made the base gluten-free to match. As the recipe makes a lot, these bars would be perfect for a party or a summer barbecue.

150g (5½oz/1⅓ sticks) unsalted butter, diced, plus extra for greasing

235g (8½oz/1¾ cups) gluten-free plain (all-purpose) flour

1 teaspoon xanthan gum (omit if your flour blend already includes it)

135g (4¾oz/⅔ cup) caster (superfine) sugar

¼ teaspoon fine sea salt

1 teaspoon vanilla extract

FOR THE TOPPING

Zest of 3 lemons

450g (1lb/2¼ cups) caster (superfine) sugar

2 tablespoons cornflour (cornstarch)

5 large eggs

3 large egg yolks

360ml (12½fl oz/1½ cups) lemon juice (about 8–9 lemons)

¼ teaspoon fine sea salt

100g (3½oz/7 tablespoons) unsalted butter, diced

Preheat the oven to 180°C (160°C Fan) 350°F, Gas Mark 4. Lightly grease your 23 x 33cm (9 x 13in) baking tin and line with a large single sheet of parchment paper that fully covers both base and sides.

Add the butter to a small pan and melt over a low heat.

Meanwhile, place the flour, xanthan gum (if using), sugar and salt in a large bowl and mix together. Pour in the melted butter and the vanilla, then stir together with a butter knife until a uniform dough forms. Scrape the dough into the prepared tin and press into an even layer. Dock the surface with a fork, then place the tin in the freezer for about 10 minutes, or until firm.

Bake for 30–35 minutes, or until golden brown. Set aside for the moment, but leave the oven on.

For the topping, place the lemon zest and sugar in a large saucepan and rub together with your fingers until the mixture smells fragrant and has the texture of wet sand. Using a balloon whisk, mix in the cornflour, followed by the eggs and egg yolks, and then the lemon juice and salt. Place the pan over a medium heat and cook, whisking constantly, until the mixture starts to bubble and thicken.

Remove the pan from the heat and stir in the butter until melted. Pour the mixture through a sieve onto the still-warm base and return the tin to the oven. Bake for about 15 minutes, or until the edges are set and the middle has a gelatinous wobble; it should jiggle like jelly (jello), not like liquid. Set aside to cool for 1 hour before transferring to the refrigerator for at least 4 hours.

Use the parchment paper to carefully lift the bars from the tin, then use a sharp knife to cut into small squares. Dust with icing sugar if you wish, but do so just before serving, as it dissolves if left sitting for too long.

If stored in a sealed container and refrigerated, the bars will keep for about 3 days.

WAGON WHEEL BARS

MAKES 16

Why is it that the things we love as children often disappoint us as adults? Case in point, wagon wheels (similar to moon pies for my friends across the Atlantic), which I loved as a kid. My curiosity as to how they'd taste now led me to buying some a couple of years back and being sorely disappointed. They were dry and cardboard-like and not at all how I remembered them. These incredibly simple bars – crisp biscuit, generously topped with jam, marshmallow and a thick layer of chocolate – are my homage to the memory, if not the reality, of that childhood favourite.

150g (5½oz/1⅓ sticks) unsalted butter, diced, plus extra for greasing

235g (8½oz/1¾ cups + 2 tablespoons) plain (all-purpose) flour

135g (4¾oz/⅔ cup) caster (superfine) sugar

¼ teaspoon fine sea salt

1 teaspoon vanilla extract

FOR THE FILLING

200g (7oz/½ cup + 2 tablespoons) raspberry jam

200g (7oz) mini marshmallows

240g (8½oz) chocolate (I use a mix of dark and milk), roughly chopped

30g (1oz/2 tablespoons) unsalted butter

Preheat the oven to 180°C (160°C Fan) 350°F, Gas Mark 4. Lightly grease your 23 x 33cm (9 x 13in) baking tin and line with a strip of parchment paper that overhangs the long sides, securing it in place with metal clips.

Add the butter to a small pan and place over a low heat until melted.

Meanwhile, combine the flour, sugar and salt in a large bowl. Pour in the melted butter and the vanilla and stir with a butter knife until a dough forms. Scrape the dough into the prepared tin and spread evenly. Dock the surface with a fork, then place the tin in the freezer for about 10 minutes, or until firm.

Bake for 30–35 minutes, or until golden brown. Allow to cool for a couple of minutes before spreading with the jam. Sprinkle the marshmallows evenly over the top.

Heat the grill (broiler) to high. Place the tin under the grill for 30–45 seconds, or until the marshmallows are puffed up and very lightly golden. Set aside.

Place the chocolate and butter in a heatproof bowl and melt in a microwave, using short bursts of heat to prevent it from burning, or set over a pan of simmering water (ensuring the bowl doesn't actually touch the water). Scrape the chocolate mixture onto the marshmallows and spread evenly. Refrigerate until the chocolate has set.

Use the parchment paper to carefully lift the bars from the tin, then use a fine sharp knife to cut into pieces. If you want neat slices, you can warm the knife in hot water, wiping it dry before using, to help cut through the chocolate without cracking it.

Stored in a sealed container, these bars will keep for 3–4 days.

MISO AND RYE CHOCOLATE CHIP COOKIE BARS

MAKES 12–15

Miso might not be a traditional cookie ingredient, but once you've tried it, you'll understand my love for these bars. The miso gives a subtle savoury flavour, an almost buttery note, to the dough, and helps make the cookies a sweet and salty delight. The rye flour also helps to create an undeniably delectable cookie.

225g (8oz/1 cup) vegan butter, plus extra for greasing

200g (7oz/⅔ cup + 2 tablespoons) light brown sugar

150g (5½oz/¾ cup) caster (superfine) sugar

2 vegan eggs

2 heaped tablespoons white miso paste

1 teaspoon vanilla extract

300g (10½oz/2⅓ cups + 1 tablespoon) plain (all-purpose) flour

100g (3½oz/1 cup) wholemeal (wholegrain) rye flour

½ teaspoon fine sea salt

¾ teaspoon bicarbonate of soda (baking soda)

¾ teaspoon baking powder

300g (10½oz) milk or dark vegan chocolate, roughly chopped

Sea salt flakes, for sprinkling

Lightly grease your 23 x 33cm (9 x 13in) baking tin and line with a strip of parchment paper that overhangs the long sides, securing it in place with metal clips.

Place the vegan butter and sugars in a large bowl and beat with an electric mixer for about 5 minutes, until light and fluffy. Add the vegan eggs and mix until fully combined. Add the miso and vanilla and mix briefly to combine.

In a separate bowl, whisk together the flours, salt, bicarbonate of soda and baking powder. Add this dry mixture to the butter mixture and beat on a low speed just until the flour is incorporated. Add the chocolate and mix briefly until evenly distributed.

Scrape the dough into the prepared tin and spread into an even layer. Refrigerate for at least 2 hours before baking, although if you can wait, the dough will only improve by resting for a day. This helps the flour to hydrate, giving a better texture, and also improves the browning, giving a deeper final flavour.

Preheat the oven to 180°C (160°C Fan) 350°F, Gas Mark 4.

Sprinkle with a little flaked sea salt and bake for 30–35 minutes, or until the dough is golden and the edges are puffy. Set aside to cool completely in the tin.

Use the parchment paper to carefully lift the bars from the tin, then use a fine sharp knife to cut into pieces.

Stored in a sealed container, these bars will keep for 3–4 days.

NOTE This dough also makes wonderful individual cookies. Simply chill the dough as above, then divide it into 60g (2¼oz) pieces and roll them into balls. Bake on lined baking trays (cookie sheets) for about 16 minutes.

HAZELNUT AND MILK CHOCOLATE BISCOTTI

MAKES 20–25

I love soft and tender cookies, but sometimes you need something that can be dunked into a big mug of coffee, an elevenses treat, and nothing works better than a classic biscotti. This version, made with gluten-free flour, uses the perfect pairing of milk chocolate and hazelnuts, making that mug of coffee an extra special treat.

300g (10½oz/2⅛ cups) gluten-free flour, plus extra for dusting

¾ teaspoon baking powder

150g (5½oz/¾ cup) caster (superfine) sugar

30g (1oz/2 tablespoons) unsalted butter, melted

Zest of 1 large orange

2 large eggs

100g (3½oz/¾ cup) toasted hazelnuts

250g (9oz) milk chocolate, melted

Cacao nibs, for sprinkling

Preheat the oven to 200°C (180°C Fan) 400°F, Gas Mark 6. Line the base of your 23 x 33cm (9 x 13in) baking tin with parchment paper.

Place the flour, baking powder and sugar in a large bowl and mix to combine. Make a well in the middle and add the melted butter, orange zest, eggs, vanilla and hazelnuts and stir to form a firm dough. Tip it onto a well-floured work surface and cut in half. Roll each half into a sausage shape roughly 20cm (8in) long. Place in the prepared tin and press flat so that each 'sausage' is roughly 5cm (2in) wide.

Bake for 25–30 minutes, or until golden brown. Set aside to cool for 5–10 minutes. Reduce the oven temperature to 180°C (160°C Fan) 350°F, Gas Mark 4.

Carefully transfer the biscotti logs to a board and use a serrated knife to cut each into thin diagonal slices about 2.5cm (1in) thick. Place the biscotti, cut-side down, back in the tin and bake for a further 15 minutes, or until dried out and golden. Set aside to cool completely.

Pour the melted chocolate into a glass and dip the biscotti halfway in. Let the excess chocolate drip back into the glass, then place the biscotti on a sheet of parchment paper. Sprinkle the chocolate areas with cocoa nibs, then chill until the chocolate has set.

Stored in a sealed container, the biscotti will keep for up to a week.

FIVE-INGREDIENT BAKES

The recipes in this chapter use just five ingredients,
not inclusive of the following store cupboard ingredients
which are basics every baker should always have on hand.
In the recipes these ingredients are noted in italics.

BAKING POWDER
BICARBONATE OF SODA (BAKING SODA)
SEA SALT
VANILLA EXTRACT
WATER

SESAME MILK CHOCOLATE SHORTBREAD

MAKES 20

Shortbread has to be the ultimate simple bake, as it uses only a handful of ingredients and is incredibly quick and easy to make, especially if you use a food processor (as I do). The recipe is based on the ratio of 1–2–3: 1 part sugar, 2 parts butter and 3 parts flour. Once you've mastered the basic recipe, you open the door to endless variations.

190g (6¾oz/1½ cups) plain (all-purpose) flour

65g (2½oz/¼ cup + 1 tablespoon) caster (superfine) sugar

½ teaspoon fine sea salt

125g (4½oz/1 stick + 1 tablespoon) vegan butter, at room temperature, diced

60g (2¼oz/¼ cup) sesame seeds

150g (5½oz) vegan milk or dark chocolate, melted

Place the flour, sugar and salt in a food processor fitted with the blade attachment, and pulse until combined. Add the vegan butter and pulse just until the mixture starts to form a breadcrumb-like texture. Add the sesame seeds and pulse briefly, just until the dough starts to clump together.

Tip the dough onto a lightly floured work surface and use your hands to bring it together as a smooth dough. Press into a flat rectangle and wrap in clingfilm (plastic wrap). Refrigerate for about 30 minutes.

Preheat the oven to 190ºC (170ºC Fan) 375ºF, Gas Mark 5. Line the base of your 23 x 33cm (9 x 13in) baking tin with a sheet of parchment paper.

Place the chilled dough on a lightly floured work surface and roll into a rectangle roughly 16 x 20cm (6½ x 8in). Cut into 4cm (1½in) squares and transfer to the prepared tin in 5 rows of 4.

Bake for about 20 minutes, or until lightly browned around the edges. Allow to cool in the tin.

To finish, dip the shortbread squares halfway into the melted chocolate and place on a tray or board lined with parchment paper. Transfer to the refrigerator until set.

Stored in a sealed container, the shortbread will keep for 3 days.

SIMPLE POUND CAKE AND FOUR WAYS TO SERVE IT

SERVES 12–15

Everyone needs to have a good pound cake recipe in their repertoire, as it's a moist, tender and buttery blank canvas that lends itself to so many ideas. Although simple, it's a perennial favourite – cake as comfort. Enjoy it unadorned with a cup of tea, or dress it up to serve as a fancy dessert for a special occasion.

225g (8oz/2 sticks) unsalted butter, at room temperature, plus extra for greasing

400g (14oz/2 cups) caster (superfine) sugar

4 large eggs

250g (9oz/2 cups) plain (all-purpose) flour

2 teaspoons baking powder

½ teaspoon fine sea salt

80ml (3fl oz/⅓ cup) sour cream

2 teaspoons vanilla extract

Preheat the oven to 180ºC (160ºC Fan) 350ºF, Gas Mark 4. Lightly grease your 23 x 33cm (9 x 13in) baking tin and line with a strip of parchment paper that overhangs the long sides, securing it in place with metal clips.

Place the butter and sugar in a large bowl and beat with an electric mixer for about 5 minutes, until light and fluffy. Add the eggs one at a time, beating until each is incorporated before adding the next. Add the flour, baking powder and salt and mix just until combined. Add the sour cream and vanilla and mix until a smooth batter forms. Scrape the batter into the prepared tin and spread evenly.

Bake for 30–35 minutes, or until the cake is golden and springs back to a light touch. Set aside to cool completely in the tin.

Use the parchment paper to carefully lift the cake from the tin and serve, perhaps in one of the following ways.

SERVING IDEAS

GRILLED POUND CAKE

Make a simple cherry compote by heating 200g (7oz) halved and pitted cherries with 50g (1¾oz/7 tablespoons) sugar and a few drops of almond extract until the cherries have released their liquid and it has reduced to a slightly syrupy consistency. Grill two thin slices of pound cake per person and serve with the compote and sour cream or crème fraîche.

LAYER CAKE

Cut the cake into two pieces and sandwich together with your favourite buttercream.

TRIFLE

The pound cake can be cut into squares and used instead of sponge fingers (see trifle recipe, page 146).

BANANA SPLIT

Combine cubed pound cake with sliced bananas, whipped cream, vanilla ice cream and a generous drizzle of dulce de leche. This is a great way to use up leftover cake.

BROWN SUGAR TAHINI SCOTCHEROOS

MAKES 16–24

Scotcheroos are the American equivalent of the UK's rice crispy cakes, but instead of chocolate, the puffed rice is usually bound with peanut butter, corn syrup and sugar. In my take on this classic treat, the rice is bound with light brown sugar and tahini, which give a warm, nutty flavour that slightly offsets the sweetness. My liquid sweetener of choice is golden syrup for its caramel-like flavour, but corn syrup or honey will work too.

245g (8¾oz/1 cup) tahini

320g (11¼oz/1 cup) golden syrup, corn syrup or honey

220g (8oz/1 cup) light brown sugar

½ teaspoon fine sea salt

200g (7oz/6 cups) puffed rice cereal

300g milk chocolate, roughly chopped (see note below)

Sesame seeds, for sprinkling (optional)

Lightly grease your 23 x 33cm (9 x 13in) baking tin and line with a large single sheet of parchment paper that fully covers both base and sides.

Place the tahini, golden syrup, sugar and salt in a saucepan over a low heat and warm until everything is fully combined and liquid.

Place the puffed rice in a separate bowl, pour in the tahini mixture and stir straight away with a wooden spoon. (The mixture cools and stiffens quickly, so have your spoon ready to stir as soon as the tahini is added.)

Scrape the mixture into the prepared tin and press into an even layer. If the mixture becomes too hard to work, wet your hands to help with the pressing. Place the tin in the refrigerator for at least an hour, until set.

Put the chocolate in a heatproof bowl and melt in a microwave, using short bursts of heat to prevent it from burning, or set over a pan of simmering water. Pour it over the chilled scotcheroos and spread evenly. Sprinkle with sesame seeds if you like, then refrigerate until set.

Use the parchment paper to lift the scotcheroos out of the tin, and cut into small pieces while still cold. You can enjoy the bars straight from the refrigerator, when they will be firm and chewy, or at room temperature, when they'll be a little softer and stickier.

If stored in a sealed container and refrigerated, these bars will keep for up to a week.

NOTE If you want to make the scotcheroos vegan, replace the milk chocolate with dark chocolate, or use a vegan product instead. Be sure to choose puffed rice that is made without malt extract (most supermarket own brands are made without and therefore gluten-free).

BLUEBERRY LEMONADE SCONES

MAKES 12

Here's an incredibly easy way to make scones, with fizzy lemonade or Sprite, making the dough incredibly light and fluffy, and also doing the job of sweetening it. You can make the scones with any flavourings you want, but I like to keep it simple with fresh blueberries. As with any scones worth their salt, these are best split in half and served with jam and cream.

375g (13¼oz/3 cups) plain (all-purpose) flour, plus extra for dusting

4 teaspoons baking powder

½ teaspoon fine sea salt

240ml (8½fl oz/1 cup) double (heavy) cream, plus extra for brushing

240ml (8½fl oz/1 cup) fizzy lemonade or Sprite

300g (10½oz/2 cups) blueberries

Preheat the oven to 200°C (180°C Fan) 400°F, Gas Mark 6. Lightly grease your 23 x 33cm (9 x 13in) baking tin and line the base with parchment paper.

Place the flour, baking powder and salt in a large bowl and whisk to combine. Make a well in the middle and pour in the cream, lemonade and blueberries. Stir together with a butter knife, just until a soft dough forms. Scrape onto a well-floured work surface and knead once or twice to bring the dough together. Lightly flour the top of the dough, then press into a circle about 2.5cm (1in) thick. Use a 7cm (3in) round cookie cutter, dipped in flour to prevent sticking, to stamp out as many circles as possible (you should get about 8 or 9 on the first go). Gently knead the scraps of dough together, press into a circle again, then stamp out more scones. You should get a total of 12.

Place the scones in the prepared tin – they'll be nice and snug – and brush with a little extra cream.

Bake for 15–20 minutes, or until golden brown. Set aside to cool in the tin for at least 20 minutes, then turn out and carefully separate.

The scones are best served slightly warm on the day they are made, but leftovers can be stored in a sealed container for up to 2 days and rewarmed in the oven before serving.

60-SECOND CLEMENTINE CAKE

SERVES 12

I have always been a fan of moist orange cakes, the type made with ground almonds or semolina. My only issue with them is that they include a protracted period of boiling the fruit to reduce the bitterness. This version removes the need for that step, but still produces a wonderfully moist cake with just the right balance between bitter and sweet. Impressively, the batter for this can also be made in roughly 60 seconds.

500g (1lb 2oz) unwaxed clementines

8 large eggs

350g (12oz/3⅔ cups) ground almonds

300g (10½oz/1½ cups) golden caster (superfine) sugar

¾ teaspoon fine sea salt

2 teaspoons vanilla extract

4 tablespoons flaked (sliced) almonds

Preheat the oven to 180°C (160°C Fan) 350°F, Gas Mark 4. Lightly grease your 23 x 33cm (9 x 13in) baking tin and line with a large single sheet of parchment paper that fully covers both base and sides.

Peel half the clementines and discard the peel; leave the remaining clementines with the peel intact. Cut all the fruit into quarters and remove any seeds (there won't normally be any, but it's worth checking). Place in a food processor fitted with the blade attachment and process for 45 seconds, or until smooth. Add the eggs, ground almonds, sugar, salt and vanilla and process for a further 15 seconds, until a smooth batter forms.

Pour the batter into the prepared tin and spread evenly. Scatter the flaked almonds over the top, then bake for 35–40 minutes, or until the cake feels firm to the touch. Transfer to a wire rack and let it cool completely in the tin.

Once the cake has cooled, use the parchment to carefully lift it from the tin to a serving platter. Cut into slices and serve with extra clementine segments and a dollop of very lightly sweetened whipped cream.

Stored in a sealed container, this moist cake will keep for 3–4 days.

CHOCOLATE HONEY NUT BAKLAVA

MAKES ABOUT 50 SMALL PIECES

The combination of crisp pastry, chocolate and nuts all soaked in a honey syrup is a wonderful concoction. While I have kept things simple, making the baklava with any variety of nuts (a mix of almonds and pistachios being my favourite), cocoa powder and filo, you can also add spices to introduce another layer of flavour, cinnamon and cardamom being the two I would opt for. This deliciously decadent treat just cries out to be paired with strong Turkish coffee.

16 sheets of filo pastry

150g (5½oz/1⅓ sticks) unsalted butter, melted

300g (10½oz/2⅛ cups) nuts, whatever type or mixture you prefer, plus extra for serving

3 tablespoons cocoa powder

¼ teaspoon fine sea salt

240ml (8½fl oz/1 cup) honey

240ml (8½fl oz/1 cup) water

Preheat the oven to 200ºC (180ºC Fan) 400ºF, Gas Mark 6.

Unroll the sheets of filo and cut them to the same size as the base of your 23 x 33cm (9 x 13in) baking tin. Cover with a damp cloth to prevent them from drying out. Brush the inside of the baking tin with a little of the melted butter and place a sheet of filo in it. Brush with butter and repeat this layering process until you have 8 layers of pastry, finishing with a buttered layer.

Place the nuts in a food processor and pulse until they are finely chopped but not powdery. Add the cocoa and salt and pulse once or twice to combine. Tip the nuts over the pastry and spread evenly. Repeat the butter and filo layering until all the pastry has been used. If you have any melted butter left, pour it over the finished baklava. Use a sharp knife to cut into 50 square or diamond-shaped pieces.

Bake for about 30 minutes, or until golden.

Meanwhile, place the honey and water in a saucepan over a medium–high heat and bring to a simmer. Continue heating for about 5 minutes, or until reduced by a third. Pour into a jug and set aside. To give another flavour to the finished syrup, I often add a few slices of lemon and leave them to infuse while the baklava bakes.

When the baklava is ready, remove from the oven and slowly pour over the syrup until it has all has been absorbed. Set aside to cool completely.

To serve, sprinkle with a few extra chopped nuts.

If stored in a sealed container, the baklava will keep for about 3–5 days, although the crispness will be lost the longer it sits.

FRENCH APPLE AND PASSION FRUIT TART

SERVES 8

I hate to call this a lazy recipe, but let's be honest – this is a great cheat's recipe, as the only real work is peeling and slicing some apples. It's a spin on an apple *tarte fine*, a French boulangerie classic. Using ready-made pastry means this is a truly speedy recipe, which is great served as it is or with some vanilla ice cream. Granny Smith apples have the advantage of not browning quickly after slicing. If using less sharp apples that do brown quickly, tossing the slices in a little lemon juice will prevent this. Choose a puff pastry made with oil rather than butter to make this vegan.

375g (13¼oz) sheet of ready-rolled puff pastry (made with oil)

50g (1¾oz/½ cup) ground almonds

4 large Granny Smith apples

1½ tablespoons caster (superfine) sugar

FOR THE PASSION FRUIT GLAZE

2 passion fruit

25g (1oz/⅛ cup) caster (superfine) sugar

Preheat the oven to 190ºC (170ºC Fan) 375ºF, Gas Mark 5. Line the base of your 23 x 33cm (9 x 13in) baking tin with parchment paper.

Unroll the pastry and use it to line the tin, trimming it to size, if necessary. Sprinkle the ground almonds over it evenly, leaving a 1cm (½in) border all around the sides.

Peel, halve and core the apples, then cut them into thin slices. Arrange them in overlapping rows on top of the almonds, avoiding the border of the pastry. You can be neat or rustic, depending on your mood. The easiest method is to arrange them in straight rows, working from top to bottom, but if you want something that looks a little fancier, work from corner to corner in diagonal rows, as I have done in the picture.

Sprinkle the assembled tart with the sugar, again avoiding the pastry border.

Bake for about 25 minutes, or until the apples are starting to brown and the pastry is golden. Set aside while you make the glaze.

Cut the passion fruit in half and scoop the pulp into a small saucepan. Add the sugar and cook just until the mixture comes to a simmer. Brush the tart with this mixture while it is still warm. Serve warm or at room temperature with a scoop of vanilla ice cream.

The tart is best served on the day it is made.

NOTE Baking the tart on a pizza stone or baking steel, if you happen to have one, will give you extra crispy pastry.

SALTED LEMON TREACLE TART

SERVES 10–12

I have a soft spot for treacle tart, an old-fashioned but wonderfully comforting bake. The golden syrup gives it a caramel-like flavour, but can be overly sweet, so I like to offset this by adding lemon and salt. When it comes to the breadcrumbs used to thicken the filling, sliced white bread is fine, but a wholemeal (wholegrain) loaf, or even sourdough, will add more flavour. Whichever you choose, just make sure the bread is a little stale.

500g (1lb 2oz) shortcrust pastry, shop-bought or homemade

454g (1lb) can golden syrup or corn syrup

3 large eggs

½ teaspoon fine sea salt

Zest and juice of 1 lemon

150g (5½oz/2 cups) stale breadcrumbs

Preheat the oven to 190ºC (170ºC Fan) 375ºF, Gas Mark 5. Lightly grease your 23 x 33cm (9 x 13in) baking tin and line the base with parchment paper.

Lightly flour a work surface and roll the pastry into a large rectangle, then trim it to measure 38 x 28cm (15 x 11in). Use it to line the prepared tin, taking it up the sides. Dock the base with a fork, then refrigerate for 20 minutes, or until the pastry is firm.

Line the chilled pastry case with a crumpled piece of parchment paper that fully covers both base and sides and fill it with baking beans or rice.

Bake for about 25 minutes, then use the paper to carefully lift out the baking beans. Return the tin to the oven for 10 minutes, or until the pastry is lightly browned. Set aside while you prepare the filling.

Reduce the oven temperature to 170ºC (150ºC Fan) 325ºF, Gas Mark 3.

Place the syrup, eggs, salt, lemon zest and lemon juice in a large bowl and whisk until combined. Stir in the breadcrumbs. Pour this mixture into the pastry case and bake for 20–25 minutes, or until the filling is set around the edges with just the barest of wobbles in the middle. Set aside to cool.

Once cool, use the parchment to carefully lift it from the tin and cut into slices.

The tart is best served within a couple of days of baking.

NOTE Golden syrup, which gives this tart its unique flavour, is widely available in the UK and Commonwealth countries. Elsewhere, it is often easy to buy it online. The recipe can be made with honey instead, but it tends to be overwhelming on its own, so cut it with golden syrup, corn syrup or even a little treacle to add some bitterness; just keep the overall amount to 450g (1lb).

SWEDISH TOFFEE COOKIES

MAKES 18

These incredibly simple cookies, a version of the classic Swedish *kolasnittar* (caramel cuts), are the sort you can whip up with almost no effort, as they're made and baked in under half an hour. The dough is made with a little golden syrup, making for a lightly caramelized flavour, and the addition of salt and chocolate-coated toffee makes these seemingly 'basic' cookies anything but.

100g (3½oz/7 tablespoons) unsalted butter, at room temperature, plus extra for greasing

75g (2¾oz/¼ cup + 2 tablespoons) caster (superfine) sugar

1 tablespoon golden syrup, or corn syrup or honey

125g (4½oz/1 cup) plain (all-purpose) flour, plus extra for dusting

1 teaspoon baking powder

¼ teaspoon fine sea salt

60g (2¼oz) chocolate-coated toffee, e.g. Daim or Heath bar, chopped into small pieces

Preheat the oven to 180°C (160°C Fan) 350°F, Gas Mark 4. Lightly grease the base of your 23 x 33cm (9 x 13in) baking tin and line with parchment paper.

Place the butter, sugar and syrup in a large bowl and beat until light and fluffy, about 5 minutes.

In a separate bowl, whisk together the flour, baking powder and salt. Add this mixture to the butter bowl along with the toffee pieces and mix on a low speed until the dough just starts to come together.

Tip the dough onto a lightly floured work surface and use your hand to bring it together as a ball. Cut in half and form each piece into a sausage shape about 25cm (10in) long. Transfer them to the prepared tin, leaving enough space for them to spread, and use your hands to slightly flatten them.

Bake for about 15 minutes, or until golden. Set aside to cool for a few minutes, then transfer to a board and use a metal bench scraper or pizza wheel to slice diagonally into cookies. They have a slightly crisp yet chewy texture, and cutting them while still warm means they will hold their shape.

Stored in a sealed container, these cookies will keep for 4–5 days.

GARIBALDI BISCUITS

MAKES 14

For some reason, maybe subconscious, I have chosen to live in areas steeped in baking history. For years I lived in Bermondsey, an area of London that used to be known as Biscuit Town, where many of the UK's most popular biscuits were invented. Then I moved to an area that was a centre for large-scale commercial baking and the site of a benevolent home for former bakers. This particular recipe was invented in Biscuit Town in 1861 and named after the Italian general then much in the news. Made from two pastry layers sandwiched together with dried currants, it's not very sweet and nor is it very pretty, but I love snacking on Garibaldis with a big mug of tea.

125g (4½oz/1 cup) plain (all-purpose) flour, plus extra for dusting

¼ teaspoon fine sea salt

30g (1oz/2 tablespoons) unsalted butter, chilled and diced

30g (1oz/⅛ cup) caster (superfine) sugar, plus extra for sprinkling

2–3 tablespoons water

75g (2¾oz/½ cup + 1 tablespoon) dried currants

1 large egg white, lightly beaten

Place the flour and salt in a large bowl and mix together. Add the butter and rub into the flour until the mixture resembles breadcrumbs. Add the sugar and stir to combine. Add the water a tablespoon at a time, mixing it with a knife, and adding just enough to bring the dough together. It is on the dry side, so test that enough liquid has been added by squeezing a little of the dough in your hand – if it holds together, it's ready.

Tip the dough out onto a work surface and use your hands to bring it together into a uniform ball. Wrap it in clingfilm (plastic wrap) and refrigerate for about 1 hour.

Preheat the oven to 200ºC (180ºC Fan) 400ºF, Gas Mark 6. Line the base of your 23 x 33cm (9 x 13in) baking tin with parchment paper.

Lightly flour a work surface and roll the dough into a rectangle roughly 23 x 33cm (9 x 13in). Cut the pastry in half. Sprinkle the currants over one half and top with the other half. Roll this pastry sandwich into a rectangle about 18 x 28cm (7 x 11in). Cut in half lengthways, then cut each strip widthways into 7 rectangles about 2.5cm (1in) wide.

Place the biscuits in the prepared tin, then brush with a little beaten egg white and sprinkle liberally with sugar.

Bake for about 10 minutes, or until the biscuits are browned around the edges. Set aside to cool completely before serving.

Stored in a sealed container, the Garibaldis will keep for 2–3 days.

BROWN SUGAR RICOTTA AND OLIVE OIL CAKE

SERVES 12–16

This recipe was the result of a lack of planning. I was trying to make a classic ricotta cake, but had no lemons (the traditional flavouring) and, even more importantly, had run out of white sugar. To give the cake an alternative flavour, I used a fragrant extra virgin olive oil and light brown sugar, hoping they would make something equally good if not quite traditional. It was fantastic! The cake had the subtle fragrance of olive oil, caramel notes from the brown sugar, and an incredibly tender crumb from the ricotta. It would make a lovely breakfast served unadorned alongside a strong black coffee, or an easy dessert if dressed up with sour cream and berries.

150ml (5fl oz/½ cup + 2 tablespoons) extra virgin olive oil, plus extra for greasing

375g (13¼oz/3 cups) plain (all-purpose) flour

3 teaspoons baking powder

½ teaspoon bicarbonate of soda (baking soda)

1 teaspoon fine sea salt

500g (1lb 2oz/2¼ cups) full-fat ricotta cheese

350g (12oz/1¾ cups) sugar (see note below)

4 large eggs

Preheat the oven to 180°C (160°C Fan) 350°F, Gas Mark 4. Lightly grease your 23 x 33cm (9 x 13in) baking tin and line with a strip of parchment paper that overhangs the long sides, securing it in place with metal clips.

Place the flour, baking powder, bicarbonate of soda and salt in a large bowl and whisk together.

Place the ricotta, oil and sugar in a separate bowl and whisk until smooth. Whisk in the eggs, one at a time, until you have a smooth mixture. Add to the flour mixture and whisk briefly until a smooth batter forms. Scrape it into the prepared tin and spread evenly.

Bake for about 40 minutes, or until the cake springs back to a light touch and is coming away from the sides of the tin. Set aside to cool. When completely cooled, use the parchment paper to transfer the cake from the tin to a serving platter.

Serve with fresh berries and whipped cream, or simply on its own.

Stored in a sealed container, this will keep for 2–3 days.

NOTE The sugar used can be all light brown, all caster (superfine) sugar or any white sugar, or a combination of brown and white, depending on the flavour you are looking for.

ALMOND AND LEMON MELTAWAYS

MAKES 20

I love a cookie that can be quickly made in a food processor, and this one fits the bill, as it's made in a flash. The shortbread-style dough is made with icing (powdered) sugar, which gives the cookies a melt-in-the-mouth texture. To amplify this, the still-warm cookies are dusted with more icing sugar, like a blanket of freshly fallen snow. If you want flavours beyond what I have provided, you can play around with the nuts and citrus, add spicing to the dough, or even ground coffee or tea leaves (they work wonders).

170g (6oz/1½ sticks) unsalted butter, at room temperature, plus extra for greasing

120g (4¼oz/1 cup) icing (powdered) sugar

Zest of 1 lemon

75g (2¾oz/⅔ cup) almonds, finely chopped

210g (7½oz/1⅔ cups) plain (all-purpose) flour, plus extra for dusting

¼ teaspoon fine sea salt

Lightly grease your 23 x 33cm (9 x 13in) baking tin and line the base with parchment paper.

Place the butter, half the icing sugar and all the lemon zest in a food processor and pulse until the mixture is soft and creamy, 2 minutes or so.

Add the almonds and pulse briefly until combined. Add the flour and salt and pulse just until a dough starts to clump together. Tip it onto a lightly floured work surface and use your hands to form a smooth dough. Press into a flat rectangle, cover with cling film (plastic wrap) and refrigerate for at least 1 hour.

Preheat the oven to 180°C (160°C Fan) 350°F, Gas Mark 4.

Lightly flour a work surface and roll the chilled dough into a rectangle about 16 x 20cm (6½ x 8in). Cut into 4cm (1½in) squares and transfer to the prepared tin in 5 rows of 4. If the cookies have warmed up and feel soft, pop the tin back into the refrigerator for 15 minutes or so to firm up.

Bake for 12–15 minutes, or until the cookies are lightly golden. Set aside to cool for 10 minutes.

Place the remaining icing sugar in a bowl. Carefully lift the cookies from the tin, one at a time, and dip them in the sugar, turning to coat all sides. (It is important to do this while the cookies are still warm or the sugar will not stick to them as easily.)

Stored in a sealed container, these cookies will keep for 3–4 days.

PEANUT BUTTER BARS

MAKES 12–15

This may be the simplest recipe in the book – a slab of delicious peanut butter cookie dough that sets and is then cut up into bars and drizzled with chocolate. The oats used in the bars are ground in a food processor to form a rough, powdery flour. To keep a little texture, I also like to add some whole rolled oats. If you want even more texture, you can also add some roughly chopped peanuts.

350g (12oz/4⅓ cups) rolled oats

¾ teaspoon fine sea salt

220g (8oz/¾ cup + 2 tablespoons) smooth peanut butter

2 teaspoons vanilla extract

180ml (6¼fl oz/¾ cup) maple syrup

100g (3½oz) milk or dark chocolate, melted

Lightly grease your 23 x 33cm (9 x 13in) baking tin and line with a strip of parchment paper that overhangs the long sides, securing it in place with metal clips.

Place 75g (2¾oz/scant 1 cup) of the oats in a large bowl, add the salt and set aside.

Place the remaining oats in a food processor fitted with the blade attachment and process for 30–60 seconds, or until a powdery flour is formed. Tip this into the bowl of reserved oats and mix to combine.

Place the peanut butter, vanilla and maple syrup in a small saucepan over a medium heat, and stir occasionally until smooth. Pour this liquid over the oat mixture and stir to form a dough. Scrape it into the prepared tin and press into an even layer. Refrigerate for 2 hours, or until firm.

Use the parchment paper to carefully transfer the peanut butter slab from the tin to a board, then use a sharp knife to cut it into pieces. Drizzle with the melted chocolate and serve.

If stored in a sealed container and refrigerated, these bars will keep for at least a week.

NO BAKE TREATS

SPECULOOS CRUNCH BARS

MAKES 16–24

The phrase 'good things come to those who wait' does not apply to these bars. In fact, it should really be 'good things come to those who can't be bothered to bake'. A spin on classic refrigerator cakes, the base is a mixture of coconut oil, white chocolate and speculoos spread, mixed together with speculoos cookies, salted pretzels and salted peanuts, a real feast of sweet and salty treats. To gild the lily, the topping is a little extra chocolate. A little goes a long way with these bars, so I like to cut them into small pieces.

340g (12oz) white chocolate, roughly chopped

100g (3½oz/7 tablespoons) coconut oil

150g (5½oz/¾ cup) speculoos spread (cookie butter)

250g (9oz) speculoos (Lotus Biscoff) cookies, broken into small pieces

75g (2¾oz/½ cup) salted peanuts, roughly chopped

90g (3¼oz/2 cups) salted pretzels, roughly chopped

FOR THE TOPPING

200g (7oz) milk chocolate, roughly chopped

1 tablespoon coconut oil

Lightly grease your 23 x 33cm (9 x 13in) baking tin and line with a large single sheet of parchment paper that fully covers both base and sides.

Place the chocolate and coconut oil in a bowl set over a pan of simmering water and heat until they have melted. Add the speculoos spread, mixing until smooth. Remove from the heat and tip in the cookies, peanuts and most of the pretzels (reserving a small amount for decoration). Stir until thoroughly mixed. Scrape the mixture into the prepared tin and spread evenly. Refrigerate until set.

For the topping, melt the chocolate and coconut oil in a heatproof bowl set over a pan of simmering water, stirring to combine, then pour over the chilled base and spread evenly. Sprinkle with the reserved pretzels and refrigerate until set.

Use the parchment paper to transfer the speculoos crunch to a board, then use a sharp knife to cut it into pieces.

If stored in a sealed container and refrigerated, these bars will keep for about a week.

SUMMER MANGO TIRAMISU

SERVES 8–10

Clearly, this is not a classic tiramisu, but it does owe its form and construction to that Italian dish, and it feels like a nice fruity alternative to the traditional version. In place of the usual chocolate and coffee, I have used a vibrant mixture of mango, passion fruit and lime, but have kept everything else fairly similar. It is a great summer dessert, but do be sure to use mangoes at the peak of their season for the best flavour and texture.

160ml (5½fl oz/⅔ cup) fresh orange juice

80ml (3fl oz/⅓ cup) Cointreau or other orange liqueur

Juice of 1 lime

2 passion fruit

400g (14oz) sponge fingers

FOR THE MASCARPONE CREAM

500g (1lb 2oz/2¼ cups) mascarpone

240ml (8½fl oz/1 cup) double (heavy) cream

4 large egg yolks

2 teaspoons vanilla bean paste

FOR THE FRUIT FILLING

2 large mangoes

2 passion fruit

300g (10½oz) raspberries

Zest of 1 lime

Combine the orange juice, Cointreau and lime juice in a shallow bowl. Scoop the pulp of one of the passion fruit into a fine mesh sieve and press with the back of a spoon to release the juice into the Cointreau mixture. Set aside.

For the mascarpone cream, place all the ingredients in a large bowl and whisk together until smooth and just about starting to hold its shape, but not yet soft peaks.

For the fruit filling, cut the cheeks from the mangoes and use a large spoon to scoop the flesh away from the peel. Cut these cheeks into thin lengthways strips. Cut away any more of the fruit you can get from the stone and dice it.

To assemble, soak each sponge finger in the Cointreau mixture for a few seconds before arranging them in your 23 x 33cm (9 x 13in) baking tin, breaking them into pieces as necessary to cover the bottom. Spread half the cream mixture over the sponges, then top with half the mango, using the offcuts first and reserving the nicest slices for decoration. Repeat to create a second layer, then top with the reserved mango, the pulp from the second passion fruit, the raspberries and the lime zest. Refrigerate for 2 hours before serving.

Once assembled, the tiramisu can be refrigerated for up to a day.

CHOCOLATE CHIP COOKIE BARS

MAKES 12

Who doesn't love cookie dough? We know we aren't supposed to eat it raw, but who can resist? This recipe is for those cravings, but made safe, so no raw flour or uncooked eggs, just oat flour. The other benefit of these bars is that they keep for at least a week in the refrigerator, so they're always on hand when a treat is required.

115g (4oz/1 stick) unsalted butter, at room temperature, plus extra for greasing

220g (8oz/1 cup) light brown sugar

2 teaspoons vanilla extract

¼ teaspoon fine sea salt

250g (9oz/2¾ cups) gluten-free oat flour

130g (4¾oz) mini chocolate chips

FOR THE TOPPING

170g (6oz) milk chocolate, roughly chopped

30g (1oz/2 tablespoons) unsalted butter

Lightly grease your 23 x 33cm (9 x 13in) baking tin and line with a strip of parchment paper that overhangs the long sides, securing it in place with metal clips.

Place the butter and sugar in a large bowl and beat with an electric mixer until light and fluffy, about 5 minutes. Add the vanilla and beat to combine. Add the salt, oat flour and chocolate chips and mix until a dough forms. Scrape it into the prepared tin and press into an even layer. Refrigerate while you make the topping.

Melt the chocolate, either in a microwave, using short bursts of heat to prevent it from burning, or in a heatproof bowl set over a pan of simmering water (ensuring that the bottom of the bowl doesn't touch the water). Remove from the heat, add the butter and stir together until smooth. Pour the chocolate mixture over the dough in the tin and spread evenly. Refrigerate for 2 hours, or until set.

Use the parchment paper to transfer the chilled slab to a board, then use a fine sharp knife to cut it into 12 pieces.

If stored in a sealed container and refrigerated, these bars will keep for at least a week.

NO BAKE TREATS

BLOOD ORANGE VANILLA GRANITA

SERVES 6–8

Granita is one of those desserts that almost makes itself, an incredibly low-effort affair that is a great option if you're already busy making the rest of the meal. While the granita itself is wonderfully simple, it can easily be dressed up and turned into a special dessert. With this blood orange version, I like to serve it alongside cake offcuts, or sponge fingers, or even amaretti, topped with a big dollop of white chocolate whipped cream and drizzled with a little bitter Campari.

400ml (14fl oz/1⅔ cups) blood orange juice

75g (2¾oz/¼ cup + 2 tablespoons) caster (superfine) sugar

1 teaspoon vanilla bean paste

Place the blood orange juice, sugar and vanilla in a saucepan over a low heat and warm just until the sugar has dissolved. Pour this mixture into the baking tin and freeze for about 2 hours, mixing it with a fork every 30 minutes or so to prevent it from freezing into a solid block. This frequent agitation prevents the ice crystals becoming too large and making it taste overly icy.

Once the granita is formed and there is no liquid remaining, pop the tin back in the freezer until you're ready to serve. Once frozen, it is best served within a few hours, but can be made up to a couple days in advance if necessary. In this case, you may find it needs scraping with a fork before serving to break up any big ice clumps that might have formed.

CORNFLAKE CRUNCH BARS

SERVES 12–15

As a kid, I was a big fan of making and eating cornflake or puffed rice cakes, a simple mixture of chocolate and cereal stirred together and allowed to set. Sweet and crunchy, what's not to like? These bars are based on that simple pleasure, but made when you want something almost as easy but with a lot more going on – cornflake cakes made fancy. To reduce the sweetness a little, and get more flavour into these bars, I like to use caramelized white chocolate, but if that's unavailable, or you can't be bothered to make any, normal white chocolate will be fine.

60g (2¼oz/4 tablespoons) unsalted butter, plus extra for greasing

200g (7oz) caramelized white chocolate, roughly chopped

3 tablespoons golden syrup or clear honey

125g (4½oz/5 cups) cornflakes, plus a handful extra for sprinkling

75g (2¾oz/⅔ cup) salted peanuts, roughly chopped

FOR THE FILLING AND TOPPING

250g (9oz/1 cup) smooth peanut butter, at room temperature

200g (7oz) dark chocolate (65–75% cocoa solids), roughly chopped

45g (1½oz/3 tablespoons) unsalted butter

Lightly grease your 23 x 33cm (9 x 13in) baking tin and line with a large single sheet of parchment paper that fully covers both base and sides.

Place the chocolate, butter and golden syrup in a large heatproof bowl set over a pan of simmering water and allow to melt, stirring occasionally. If the mixture looks like it is separating, use a whisk to stir until smooth and thick. Remove from the heat and add the cornflakes and peanuts, stirring until evenly mixed. As you do this, the cornflakes will break into smaller pieces, but that's fine. Scrape this mixture into the prepared tin and compact into a flat, even layer. Refrigerate until set.

For the filling, spread the peanut butter over the chilled base in a thin, even layer. Refrigerate for about 1 hour.

For the topping, melt the chocolate and butter in a heatproof bowl set over a pan of simmering water. Alternatively, melt in a microwave, using short bursts of heat to prevent it from burning. Once fully melted, set the bowl aside to cool slightly, before pouring the mixture over the peanut butter and spreading evenly. Sprinkle with the extra cornflakes, then refrigerate until set.

Use the parchment paper to carefully transfer the chocolate crunch to a board, then use a sharp knife to cut into 12–15 bars.

If stored in a sealed container and refrigerated, these bars will keep for 4–5 days.

NOTE While corn is naturally gluten-free, some brands of cornflakes (Kellogg's among them) also include malt, a wheat derivative. Fortunately, many own brands and organic brands are gluten-free, but do check the ingredients list on the packet if making these bars for someone who is on a gluten-free diet.

CHOCOLATE MOUSSE TART

SERVES 10–12

Chocolate mousse is a death row dessert for me; it's no fuss, simple and straightforward, just light chocolate goodness with maybe a little cream to sweeten the deal. In the past, the vegan chocolate mousse recipes I tried didn't pass my basic mousse test: they were creamy and dense rather than light and fluffy. My version here is light, as it should be, and since it doesn't use any dairy, it has a clarity of flavour. The chocolate is the star of the show, so use a brand you love.

300g (10½oz) dark chocolate (65–75% cocoa solids), finely chopped

180ml (6¼fl oz/¾ cup) aquafaba (the liquid from a 400g/14oz can of chickpeas/garbanzos)

¼ teaspoon cream of tartar

75g (2¾oz/⅓ cup) light brown sugar

1 teaspoon vanilla bean paste

120ml (4fl oz/½ cup) soya milk

Cocoa powder, for dusting

FOR THE COOKIE CRUST

36 Oreo-style cookies, including the filling (see note below)

85g (3oz/⅔ cup) vegan butter, melted

Large pinch of salt

NOTE Oreo-branded cookies are no longer classified as vegan, but many similar-style cookies, often supermarket own brands, do qualify as vegan. To be on the safe side, read the information on the packaging.

Line your 23 x 33cm (9 x 13in) baking tin with a large single sheet of foil, pressing it into the sides and corners so it sits flush in the tin and covers all sides.

For the crust, place the Oreos in a food processor fitted with the blade attachment and process for a minute or so, until finely ground. Add the melted vegan butter and salt and process until combined.

Scrape the mixture into the prepared tin and spread evenly. Using your hands, press down on the base and push some of it up the sides to create a lip about 2.5cm (1in) high. Use a measuring cup or the base of a glass to compact the crust to make it secure. Freeze until needed.

For the mousse, put the chocolate in a large heatproof bowl and melt in a microwave, using short bursts of heat to prevent it from burning, or place it over a pan of simmering water (ensuring the bowl does not touch the water). Set aside to cool.

Place the aquafaba and cream of tartar in a large bowl and use an electric mixer to whisk at medium–high speed until the mixture holds stiff peaks and doesn't slip around the bowl when turned upside down; about 5–10 minutes.

With the mixer running, very slowly add the sugar a spoonful at a time, whisking very well between each addition. Once the sugar has been incorporated, continue whisking until it has fully dissolved and you have a stiff meringue. Add the vanilla and whisk briefly to combine.

Pour the soya milk into the chocolate and stir until smooth. Add a quarter of the meringue and fold it into the chocolate. Once combined, fold in the remaining meringue in two further additions, taking care not to overmix so that the mousse remains as light as possible.

Scrape the mousse into the chilled crust and spread evenly. Refrigerate for 2 hours, or until set. Serve the tart straight from the refrigerator, dusted with cocoa powder.

Store in a sealed container in the fridge for 1–2 days.

SALTED PISTACHIO AND ROSE BRITTLE

SERVES 10

Pistachio and rose is one of my favourite flavour combinations, and it makes this simple brittle feel grown up and sophisticated. A great edible gift, it is the sort of simple sweet that you go back to nibble on until you wonder where it all went. The process of making brittle is similar to that for toffee and honeycomb (cinder toffee), the difference being in the ratios of fat and the amounts of bicarbonate of soda (baking soda). Once you've learned to make one, you can be confident in making any of them. While candy-making can seem daunting, if you follow the temperatures given, it's very easy and a fun project.

60g (2¼oz/4 tablespoons) vegan butter, plus extra for greasing

250g (9oz/2 cups) shelled pistachios

150g (5½oz/¾ cup) caster (superfine) sugar

225g (8oz/⅔ cup) golden syrup or brown rice syrup

1 tablespoon water

1 tablespoon rose water

¼ teaspoon bicarbonate of soda (baking soda)

1–2 tablespoons edible rose petals (optional)

½ teaspoon flaked sea salt

Lightly grease your 23 x 33cm (9 x 13in) baking tin and line with a large single sheet of parchment paper that fully covers both base and sides.

Take about 50g (1¾oz/scant ½ cup) of the pistachios, roughly chop them and set aside for decoration.

Place the butter, sugar, syrup and water in a large, heavy-based saucepan over a medium heat, stirring occasionally, until it reaches 149°C (300°F) on an instant-read or jam thermometer. Remove from the heat, add the whole pistachios and rose water and stir to combine. The mixture will thicken up immediately, so place it back on the heat and stir until it becomes liquid and again reaches 149°C (300°F). Remove from the heat and add the bicarbonate of soda, mixing until combined. Quickly tip the mixture into the prepared tin and spread evenly. Sprinkle immediately with the chopped pistachios, the rose petals (if using) and the salt.

Set the tin aside for a couple of hours, until firm. Remove the brittle from the tin, then use a rolling pin to break into pieces.

Stored in a sealed container in a cool, dry spot, the brittle should keep for at least a week.

ALMOND BUTTER SPICED POPCORN BARS

MAKES 16

I love cinema popcorn – I'll take a sweet and salty mix, please – but for home movie nights I sometimes want something a little different. These bars, inspired by masala chai, my favourite hot drink on a cold winter's day, are packed full of warming spices and bursting with texture.

100g (3½oz/7 tablespoons) coconut oil, plus extra for greasing

60ml (2¼ fl oz/¼ cup) honey

75g (2¾oz/⅓ cup) light brown sugar

1 teaspoon ground cinnamon

1 teaspoon ground ginger

¼ teaspoon ground cardamom

¼ teaspoon ground nutmeg

Pinch of freshly ground black pepper

185g (6½oz/¾ cup) smooth almond butter

70g (2½oz/7 cups) lightly salted popcorn

85g (3oz/⅔ cup) raisins

50g (1¾oz/½ cup) pecans, roughly chopped

Lightly grease your 23 x 33cm (9 x 13in) baking tin and line with a large single sheet of parchment paper that fully covers both base and sides.

Place the coconut oil in a saucepan with the honey, sugar and spices and set over a medium heat until everything has melted and is just starting to bubble. Remove from the heat and stir in the almond butter.

Put the popcorn, raisins and pecans into a very large bowl and toss to combine. Pour over the almond butter mixture and stir until everything is evenly coated. Scrape this mixture into the prepared tin and spread evenly, then use the base of a glass or measuring cup to compact it firmly. Refrigerate for a few hours, or until set.

Use the parchment to transfer the slab to a board, then use a large, sharp knife to cut it into 16 equal pieces.

If stored in a sealed container and refrigerated, these bars will keep for 2–3 days.

HAZELNUT ROCHER CHEESECAKES

SERVES 12–15

As a child of the 1980s, I always considered Ferrero Rocher chocolates the height of sophistication. The adverts declared them worthy of an ambassador's black tie soirée, and I bought into the fantasy. My no bake *rochers* (rocks) are a cross between cheesecake and a choc-ice (Klondike Bar), another childhood favourite. The frozen cheesecake is coated in a milk chocolate shell that hardens almost immediately, a fun textural element that is reminiscent of those gold-wrapped chocolates.

250g (9oz) speculoos (Lotus Biscoff) cookies

50g (1¾oz/⅓ cup) toasted hazelnuts

¼ teaspoon fine sea salt

85g (3oz/6 tablespoons) unsalted butter, melted

FOR THE CHEESECAKE

240ml (8½fl oz/1 cup) double (heavy) cream, chilled

1 teaspoon vanilla bean paste

700g (1lb 8½oz/3⅛ cups) full-fat cream cheese, at room temperature

120g (4¼oz/1 cup) icing (powdered) sugar

150g (5½oz/½ cup) chocolate hazelnut spread, at room temperature

¼ teaspoon fine sea salt

FOR THE SHELL

170g (6oz) milk chocolate, roughly chopped

45ml (1¾fl oz/⅛ cup + 1 tablespoon) coconut oil

100g (3½oz/¾ cup) toasted hazelnuts, finely chopped

Lightly grease your 23 x 33cm (9 x 13in) baking tin and line with a large single sheet of parchment paper that fully covers both base and sides.

Add the cookies, hazelnuts and salt to a food processor fitted with the blade attachment and pulse until ground to fine crumbs. Pour in the melted butter and pulse until evenly mixed. Scrape the mixture into the prepared tin and use the base of a glass or measuring cup to compact evenly. Set aside.

For the cheesecake, put the cream and vanilla into a large bowl and whisk into soft peaks. Set aside.

Put the cream cheese, icing sugar, chocolate spread and sea salt into another bowl and use an electric mixer to beat together until smooth and combined, about 2 minutes.

Add the whipped vanilla cream to the cheesecake mixture and fold together until evenly combined. Scrape this into the tin and spread evenly. Cover and place in the freezer until the cheesecake is solid, about 4 hours.

For the shell, melt the chocolate and coconut oil in a heatproof bowl in a microwave, using short bursts of heat to prevent it from burning, or over a pan of simmering water. Once melted, stir in the chopped hazelnuts, then set aside for at least 10 minutes before using.

To serve, use the parchment paper to carefully lift the frozen cheesecake from the tin and transfer it to a board. Cut into squares, then dip them into the chocolate mixture or simply pour a little of it on top of them. I like to serve the *rochers* while still firm from the freezer, almost like ice cream, but if you prefer, you can leave them to soften so that the cheesecake has a more mousse-like texture.

If kept frozen in a sealed container, the *rochers* will keep for about 2 weeks.

ENGLISH TOFFEE

SERVES 8

Although described as English, this style of toffee, made with chocolate and almonds, is actually more common in the US than the UK. Regardless of its true origins, the toffee is a favourite confection of mine and incredibly easy to make. Crisp and buttery, it's a wonderful treat, but also makes a great edible gift. Another good idea is to chop it up and add it to cookie dough.

225g (8oz/2 sticks) unsalted butter, plus extra for greasing

100g (3½oz/½ cup) caster (superfine) sugar

100g (3½oz/⅓ cup + 2 tablespoons) light brown sugar

¼ teaspoon fine sea salt

2 tablespoons water

85g (3oz) dark chocolate, roughly chopped

85g (3oz) toasted almonds, roughly chopped

Lightly grease your 23 x 33cm (9 x 13in) baking tin and line it with a large single sheet of parchment paper that stands slightly above all the sides.

Place the sugars and butter in a large, heavy-based saucepan over a medium heat and stir until the butter has melted. Add the salt and water and continue heating, stirring occasionally, until the mixture reaches 149°C (300°F) on an instant-read or jam thermometer. Remove immediately from the heat and pour into the prepared tin. Using oven gloves, tilt the tin so that the toffee spreads over the whole base. Allow to cool for a couple of minutes, before sprinkling the chocolate evenly over the toffee.

Set aside for a few minutes, until the chocolate has melted, then use the back of a spoon or an offset spatula to spread evenly.

While the chocolate is still melted, sprinkle over the chopped almonds. Set aside for 2 hours, until fully set.

Use the parchment paper to transfer the toffee to a board, then use a sharp knife to cut it into pieces.

Stored in a sealed container in a dark, cool spot, the toffee will keep for at least a week.

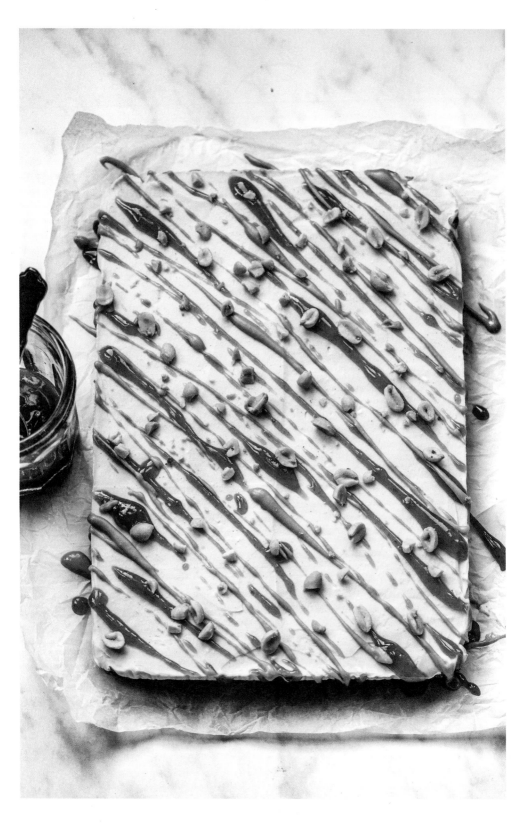

PB & J SLAB CHEESECAKE

SERVES 12

When it comes to vegan baking, I'm not sure many desserts will be as simple or as crowd-pleasing as this one. For the base, I recommend using speculoos biscuits, which happen to be vegan and also have a great toasty, almost caramelized, flavour. If you prefer, digestives or Graham crackers (both vegan) can be used instead. The great thing about this recipe is that it is set in the freezer, so it's a brilliant prepare-ahead dessert and will keep well for weeks.

750g (1lb 10½oz/3⅓ cups) vegan cream cheese (I use Violife)

170g (6oz/⅔ cup) smooth peanut butter

120g (4¼oz/1 cup) icing (powdered) sugar

1 teaspoon vanilla bean paste

¼ teaspoon fine sea salt

FOR THE BASE

85g (3oz/6 tablespoons) vegan butter or coconut oil, melted, plus extra for greasing

250g (9oz) speculoos (Lotus Biscoff) cookies

50g (1¾oz/⅓ cup) salted peanuts

FOR THE TOPPING

50g (1¾oz/3 tablespoons) smooth peanut butter

80g (2¾oz/¼ cup) raspberry jam

2 teaspoons water

2 tablespoons peanuts, roughly chopped

Lightly grease your 23 x 33cm (9 x 13in) baking tin and line with a large single sheet of parchment paper that fully covers both base and sides.

For the base, place the cookies and peanuts in a food processor and pulse until finely ground. Pour in the melted vegan butter or coconut oil and pulse until evenly mixed. Tip the mixture into the prepared tin and press into an even layer, compacting it with the base of a glass or measuring cup. Pop the tin into the refrigerator while you make the cheesecake filling.

Place the cream cheese, peanut butter, icing sugar, vanilla and salt in a large bowl and beat with an electric mixer for a minute or so, until smooth. Scrape the mixture into the tin and spread evenly. Cover with clingfilm (plastic wrap) and freeze for at least 1½ hours, until firm.

If kept frozen in a sealed container, the cheesecake will keep for up to a month.

To serve, use the parchment paper to carefully transfer the cheesecake to a platter. It can be served cold and firm straight from the freezer or allowed to thaw for a softer texture.

For the topping, gently warm the peanut butter and drizzle it over the cheesecake. Mix the jam with the water to make a pourable mixture and drizzle this over the cheesecake as well. Finish by sprinkling over the chopped peanuts.

Kept frozen, the cheesecake will keep for up to a month. If stored in a sealed container in the refrigerator, it will keep for around 4–5 days.

CHOCOLATE DIPPED HONEYCOMB

MAKES ABOUT 25–30 CHUNKS

Honeycomb (cinder toffee) is one of the easiest things to make in the kitchen, and it has the advantage of feeling like a fun science experiment. Sugar is cooked until caramelized and hot, then bicarbonate of soda (baking soda) and cream of tartar are very quickly whisked in, causing it to erupt and foam up. Poured into a tin and left to set, you are rewarded with a bittersweet honeycomb candy which, once dipped in chocolate, makes a fabulous edible gift.

Oil, for greasing

4 teaspoons bicarbonate of soda (baking soda)

½ teaspoon cream of tartar

80ml (3fl oz/⅓ cup) golden syrup or corn syrup

300g (10½oz 1½ cups) caster (superfine) sugar

300g (10½oz) dark chocolate, melted

Lightly grease your 23 x 33cm (9 x 13in) baking tin and line with a large single sheet of parchment paper that stands slightly above all the sides. Set close to your hob.

Weigh out all your ingredients before you start because this recipe happens so quickly that you won't have time to do any prep once the sugar is cooked to the right temperature.

Place the bicarbonate of soda and cream of tartar in a small bowl and stir to combine.

Scrape the syrup into a large saucepan and pour in the sugar. Place over a medium heat, stirring occasionally with a heatproof spatula, until the mixture is smooth and the sugar has dissolved. Continue heating until the mixture is a rich caramel colour and reaches 149°C (300°F) on an instant-read or jam thermometer.

Remove the pan from the heat and, using a metal whisk, very briefly mix in the bicarbonate mixture. This action needs to be quick but without leaving lumps. Overwhisking at this point will deflate the honeycomb.

Pour the honeycomb into your prepared tin and watch as it grows and expands. Set aside for a few hours or until fully set.

Put a large sheet of parchment paper on a work surface. Place the melted chocolate in a small bowl. Break the honeycomb into chunks, dip them into the chocolate, then place on the parchment paper until set.

Stored in an airtight container in a cool, dry place, the honeycomb should keep for about a week.

NO-CHURN CAPPUCCINO ICE CREAM SANDWICHES

MAKES 15–18

Is there anything better than knowing that your freezer is full of ice cream sandwiches? Whether they're for an impromptu barbecue when the sun comes out, or just for you and your family as a weekend treat, they'll bring a smile to everyone's face. The filling, a no-churn espresso ice cream, is sandwiched in a creamy white chocolate shell, so there's no baking involved. The key to making a no-churn ice cream that doesn't taste like a frozen mousse is whipping the mixture just the right amount, until it is barely holding soft peaks.

Oil, for greasing

400g (14oz) Nice biscuits or Graham crackers, or any rectangular cookie you prefer

600ml (20fl oz/2½ cups) double (heavy) cream

397g (14oz) can condensed milk

1½ teaspoons instant espresso powder

Pinch of salt

FOR THE SANDWICH SHELL

170g (6oz) white chocolate, roughly chopped

30g (1oz/2 tablespoons) coconut oil

Lightly grease your 23 x 33cm (9 x 13in) baking tin and line with a large single sheet of parchment paper that fully covers both base and sides.

Arrange half the cookies in the tin, breaking them up as necessary to cover the entire base.

Place the cream, condensed milk, espresso powder and salt in a large bowl and whisk with an electric mixer just until the mixture starts to holds soft peaks. Scrape it into the prepared tin and spread evenly. Arrange the remaining cookies on top of the ice cream.

Cover the tin with clingfilm (plastic wrap) and freeze for at least 4 hours.

Use the parchment paper to carefully transfer the frozen slab to a board. Using a sharp knife, cut it into 15–18 bars. I like to use the cookie rows as a guide for where to cut, but you can cut in any way you like. Pop the sandwiches back into the freezer while you prepare the chocolate shell.

Melt the chocolate and coconut oil in a heatproof bowl set over a pan of simmering water. Once melted, stir well to ensure everything is combined, then set aside for 10 minutes or so to cool slightly.

Place a large sheet of parchment paper on a work surface. Remove the ice cream sandwiches from the freezer and half-dip them into the chocolate mixture, allowing any excess to drip back into the bowl. The coconut oil will make the chocolate harden very quickly against the cold ice cream, so if you want to decorate with sprinkles or a little more espresso powder, do this quickly after the dipping. Set aside on the parchment paper.

The ice cream sandwiches can be served immediately, or stored in a sealed container in the freezer, where they will keep for up to 2 weeks.

CHOCOLATE BARK WITH PUFFED RICE AND SEEDS

SERVES 8

I know this recipe sounds a bit worthy, maybe even a little boring, but the exact opposite is true. The bark is made with dark chocolate mixed with puffed rice cereal and coated in a mixture of seeds, making for a delicious, crunchy treat. Take care to use brands of puffed rice that are marked as gluten-free and/or vegan, as some include malt syrup, which may contain gluten, and others have added vitamin D, which may be non-vegan in origin. Fortunately, many supermarket own brands of the cereal are made without these ingredients.

Oil, for greasing

400g (14oz) dark chocolate, roughly chopped

50g (1¾oz/2 cups) puffed rice cereal

35g (1¼oz/¼ cup) mixed seeds

½ teaspoon flaked sea salt

Lightly grease your 23 x 33cm (9 x 13in) baking tin and line it with a large single sheet of parchment paper that fully covers both base and sides.

Place the chocolate in a bowl and microwave on high for 30 seconds. Although it won't look like anything has happened, give it a good stir anyway, then repeat this step. After the second stir, repeat the microwaving, but now in 15-second bursts, until the chocolate is about three-quarters melted. Remove the bowl and stir until fully melted.

Add the cereal to the chocolate and stir until evenly coated. Scrape the mixture into the prepared tin and spread evenly. Immediately sprinkle over the seeds and salt. Refrigerate until set.

Use the parchment paper to transfer the bark to a board, then break it into chunks.

If stored in a sealed container in the refrigerator, the bark will keep for at least a week.

NOTE Melting chocolate in a microwave in this manner is a very simplified version of tempering, which ensures it is shiny and sets with a snap.

DESSERTS

FUNFETTI ARCTIC ROLL

SERVES 8–10

Arctic roll is pure nostalgia, a dessert of my childhood. This is my interpretation of the frozen-aisle treat, made vegan and with lots of sprinkles to keep the fun nostalgic edge. Traditionally, the rolled cake has a thin layer of jam separating it from the ice cream filling, which adds another flavour and a pop of colour.

120ml (4fl oz/½ cup) soya milk

½ teaspoon cider vinegar

125g (4½oz/1 cup) plain (all-purpose) flour

30g (1oz/¼ cup) icing (powdered) sugar

1 teaspoon baking powder

¼ teaspoon bicarbonate of soda (baking soda)

¼ teaspoon fine sea salt

4 tablespoons vegetable oil

120ml (4fl oz/½ cup) coconut condensed milk

2–4 tablespoons colourful sprinkles

FOR THE FILLING

2 x 475ml (1 pint) cartons of vegan ice cream

Raspberry jam (optional)

Start by making the filling. Scoop the ice cream into a large bowl and cut into small chunks; this will help it to soften quickly and more evenly. Once soft and spreadable, scrape it onto a large sheet of clingfilm (plastic wrap) and shape it into a cylinder about 20cm (8in) long. Wrap the clingfilm around it, twisting the ends, and freeze for about 2 hours, until firm. If you want the ice cream to be nice and round, take it out of the freezer when firmer but not fully frozen and roll it on a work surface, using light pressure to refine the shape.

Preheat the oven to 180ºC (160ºC Fan) 350ºF, Gas Mark 4. Lightly grease your 23 x 33cm (9 x 13in) baking tin and line with a strip of parchment paper that overhangs the long sides, securing it in place with metal clips.

To make the cake, put the soya milk in a jug, add the vinegar and stir together. Place the flour in a large bowl with the sugar, baking powder, bicarbonate of soda and salt and mix together. Make a well in the middle and pour in the milk mixture, oil and condensed milk. Mix with a whisk to form a smooth batter. Scrape it into the prepared tin and spread evenly, then scatter over the sprinkles.

Bake for 15–20 minutes, or until lightly browned. Be careful not to overbake the cake, as this makes it more likely to crack when rolled up. Set aside to cool for 5 minutes, then use the parchment paper to carefully lift the cake from the tin. Invert it onto a piece of parchment paper and gently peel off the original paper. Set aside to cool completely.

If you want to include the jam, place a few tablespoons of it in a small bowl and beat until loose, adding a little water if it's very thick. Spread a very thin layer of the jam over the cake. Unwrap the ice cream, place it along the short edge of the cake and gently roll up. Trim off any excess cake once the ice cream is fully enclosed, then freeze until ready to serve.

Kept frozen, this dessert will keep for a couple of weeks.

LEMON AND RASPBERRY TRIFLE-ISH

SERVES 8–10

A kind of Frankendessert, this is inspired by various things, the first of which is the trifle my mum makes every Christmas. It's a very traditional affair, and one of the few classic trifles I have ever enjoyed. The base layer of this recipe is inspired by that family favourite. The topping, however, is not traditional at all; it's a light and fluffy lemon mousse inspired by the Danish dessert citronfromage (despite the name, there is no cheese involved). This almost-trifle is a perfect summer dessert, as it's a no bake affair and is bright and light in flavour. While the use of gelatine and the need to make a mousse might seem daunting to some, I promise you it's a straightforward dessert that anyone can make.

200g (7oz) sponge fingers, leftover cake or amaretti biscuits

200g (7oz/⅔ cup) raspberry jam

80ml (3fl oz/⅓ cup) Amaretto liqueur

175g (6oz) raspberries

FOR THE MOUSSE

3 sheets of gelatine

3 large eggs

100g (3½oz/½ cup) caster (superfine) sugar

Zest and juice of 2 lemons

200ml (7fl oz/½ cup + ⅓ cup) double (heavy) cream

FOR THE TOPPING

480ml (2 cups) double (heavy) cream

30g (1oz/3 tablespoons) pistachios, roughly chopped

200g (7oz) raspberries

Break up the sponge fingers and tip them into your 23 x 33cm (9 x 13in) baking tin. Mix the jam and liqueur together in a bowl, then drizzle this liquid over the sponges. Add the raspberries and toss everything together until evenly coated.

For the mousse, place the gelatine in a bowl and cover with ice-cold water. Place the eggs, sugar and lemon zest in a large bowl and use an electric mixer to whisk for about 5 minutes, or until pale and fluffy. In a separate bowl, whisk the cream (no need to clean the beaters) until it just starts to hold soft peaks.

Place the lemon juice in a small saucepan and bring to a simmer. Squeeze the gelatine dry, then add it to the lemon juice and stir until melted. Drizzle this liquid into the egg mixture, whisking as you do so, but only long enough to combine, then fold in the cream. Pour this mixture over the raspberry base and spread evenly. Refrigerate for at least 4 hours, or until the mousse has set.

For the topping, lightly whisk the cream and dollop it randomly over the mousse. Sprinkle over the pistachios and raspberries and serve.

If stored in a sealed container and refrigerated, the dessert will keep for 3 days, but the sponges will soften further as they sit.

MAGIC CUSTARD CAKE

SERVES 12–15

Why is this cake magic? Well, through some kitchen wizardry, the simple batter transforms into three distinct layers as it bakes. The bottom is a dense vanilla custard, almost fudgy in texture; the middle is a just-set custard that reminds me of pastry cream; and the top layer, the most magical, is like a light génoise sponge. While this style of cake has enjoyed renewed popularity in the age of Pinterest, its actual origins are harder to track down. Some believe it is related to the French gâteau millasson, a type of flan traditionally made with cornflour (cornstarch), but there is a similar recipe dating from 1896 in *The Boston Cooking-School Cook Book* by Fannie Farmer, so it's safe to say this style of cake has a long and storied history.

8 large eggs, separated

250g (9oz/1¼ cups) caster (superfine) sugar

2 teaspoons vanilla bean paste

¼ teaspoon fine sea salt

225g (8oz/2 sticks) unsalted butter, melted and cooled

250g (9oz/2 cups) plain (all-purpose) flour

960ml (2 pints/4 cups) whole milk

TO SERVE

Icing (powdered) sugar

Fresh berries

Preheat the oven to 170°C (150°C fan) 325°F, Gas Mark 3. Line your 23 x 33cm (9 x 13in) baking tin with a large sheet of parchment paper that fully covers both base and sides.

Place the egg whites in a large bowl and whisk on a medium–high speed until they hold stiff peaks. Set aside for the moment.

Place the egg yolks, sugar, vanilla and salt in a separate large bowl and whisk until thick and pale. Pour in the melted butter and whisk until combined. Sift in the flour and whisk until smooth. Pour in the milk and whisk to form a smooth batter. Fold in the egg whites and don't worry about them being perfectly combined – a few flecks of white are fine. The batter will be very loose, but this is as it should be. Pour it into the prepared tin.

Bake for 65–75 minutes, or until golden brown and just set in the centre. Allow to cool at room temperature for 1 hour, before transferring the tin to the refrigerator and leaving overnight.

Use the parchment paper to carefully lift the chilled cake from the tin, then cut into pieces. You should be rewarded with a magic confection that has separated into three distinct layers. Dust with icing sugar and serve with fresh berries.

If stored in a sealed container and refrigerated, the cake will keep for 2–3 days.

APPLE AND BLACKBERRY CRUMBLE WITH ROLLED OATS AND HAZELNUTS

SERVES 10–12

Crumble is one of the first dishes I learned to make when I was a child; it was the dessert we had most weekends following a roast made by my mum. The crumble topping was something she seemingly made without a recipe and without fuss – it was whipped up in seconds, using just a knife to bring everything together. Simplicity is part of the dish's charm, but its comforting nature is what keeps me baking versions of it more often than most other desserts. This recipe makes a large crumble, perfect for when family is visiting, or simply when you want leftovers for breakfast – and yes, I would argue that cold crumble makes for a wonderful breakfast, if only occasionally.

900g (2lb) Granny Smith apples, peeled, cored and diced

675g (1½lb) blackberries

130g (4¾oz/⅔ cup) caster (superfine) sugar

Juice of 1 lemon

FOR THE TOPPING

200g (7oz/1½ cups + 2 tablespoons) plain (all-purpose) flour

130g (4¾oz/⅔ cup) caster (superfine) sugar

Large pinch of salt

175g (6oz/¾ cup + 1 teaspoon) chilled unsalted butter, diced

100g (3½oz/1¼ cups) rolled oats

60g (2¼oz/½ cup) roughly chopped hazelnuts

For the topping, place the flour, sugar and salt in a large bowl, add the butter and use your fingertips to rub it in until the mixture starts to clump together. Tip in the oats and hazelnuts and stir to combine, then press together to form it into a ball of dough. Wrap in clingfilm (plastic wrap) and refrigerate for about 1 hour, or until firm.

Preheat the oven to 190ºC (170ºC Fan) 375ºF, Gas Mark 5.

Tip the fruit into your 23 x 33cm (9 x 13in) baking tin and sprinkle over the sugar and lemon juice, tossing together to combine evenly. Break the crumble mixture into small chunks and scatter over the fruit. Bake for about 1 hour, or until the crumble is golden and the fruit is bubbling.

Set aside to cool slightly, before serving with custard, cream or ice cream, depending on your preference.

Leftovers can be stored in a sealed container and refrigerated for a couple days. Serve cold, or reheat in the oven and serve hot.

SELF-SAUCING GINGER PUDDING WITH MACADAMIAS AND MALT ICE CREAM

SERVES 10–12

Self-saucing puddings are culinary magic. A simple cake batter is made and then topped with the ingredients for a sauce. As the cake bakes, the sauce ingredients travel through the batter and turn into a luscious liquid, in this case a brown sugar caramel sauce. The pudding is accompanied here by a very easy no-churn ice cream.

100g (3½oz/7 tablespoons) unsalted butter, melted and cooled, plus extra for greasing

300g (10½oz/2⅓ cups + 1 tablespoon) plain (all-purpose) flour

150g (5½oz/⅔ cup) light brown sugar

4 teaspoons baking powder

1 teaspoon ground cinnamon

½ teaspoon fine sea salt

3 large eggs

200ml (7fl oz/¾ cup + 1 tablespoon) whole milk

75g (2¾oz/⅔ cup) diced candied ginger

75g (2¾oz/⅔ cup) macadamia nuts, roughly chopped

FOR THE NO-CHURN ICE CREAM

300ml (10fl oz/1¼ cups) double (heavy) cream

60g (2¼oz/3 tablespoons) malt powder (I prefer Ovaltine)

1 teaspoon vanilla bean paste

180ml (6¼fl oz/¾ cup) condensed milk

FOR THE SAUCE

175g (6oz/¾ cup + 2 teaspoons) light brown sugar

200ml (7fl oz/½ + ⅓ cup) hot water

2 tablespoons golden syrup or clear honey

1 teaspoon vanilla bean paste

1 tablespoon cornflour (cornstarch)

At least 4 hours before making the pudding, make the ice cream. In a small pan, heat 75ml (2¾fl oz/5 tablespoons) of the cream with the malt powder, whisking together to prevent lumps, and heating just until the mixture comes to a simmer. Scrape into a large bowl and add the vanilla, condensed milk and the remaining cream. Whisk this mixture until it just starts to hold soft peaks. Scrape into a freezer-safe container, then cover and freeze for at least 4 hours.

Preheat the oven to 180°C (160°C Fan) 350°F, Gas Mark 4. Lightly grease your 23 x 33cm (9 x 13in) baking tin.

Place the flour, sugar, baking powder, cinnamon and salt in a large bowl and whisk together. Pour in the melted butter, eggs and milk and whisk together briefly, just until combined. Reserve small amounts of the ginger and macadamias for garnish, then stir the rest into the batter. Scrape into the prepared tin and spread evenly. Sprinkle with the reserved ginger and macadamias.

For the sauce, put the sugar, water, golden syrup and vanilla in a bowl and whisk together. In a separate bowl, mix a little of this liquid with the cornflour to make a smooth paste. Return this to the sauce and whisk to combine. Pour the sauce very gently over the batter.

Bake for 35–40 minutes, or until the sauce has sunk under the sponge and the pudding springs back to a light touch. Allow to cool for a few minutes before serving with scoops of the malt ice cream.

The pudding is best served on the day it is made, but leftovers will keep for up to 3 days if refrigerated, and can be reheated to serve.

LAZY PIE

SERVES 12

While this pie starts life more like a crumble, with a mixture of fruit, sugar, thickener and lemon juice, it's even easier than a crumble because the topping is truly lazy. It's shop-bought puff pastry made fancy by latticing it, giving the impression that the pie took lots of time and effort, when really it was thrown together very quickly. Puff pastry generally comes in two varieties: 'all butter' and the more common kind, made with oil, which means the pastry is vegan.

450g (1lb) blueberries

900g (2lb) Granny Smith apples, peeled, cored and diced

Juice of 1 lemon

2 tablespoons cornflour (cornstarch)

250g (9oz/1¼ cups) caster (superfine) sugar

2 x 375g (13¼oz) sheets of puff pastry

2 tablespoons plant-based milk, for glazing

Demerara sugar, for sprinkling

Tip the fruit into your 23 x 33cm (9 x 13in) baking tin and drizzle over the lemon juice. Mix the cornflour and sugar in a bowl, then sprinkle the mixture over the fruit and use your hands to toss everything together.

Cut the first sheet of puff pastry into strips 5cm (2in) wide and as long as the tin. Lay these on top of the fruit, spacing them slightly apart. Cut the second sheet of pastry into 5cm (2in) strips the width of the tin. To lattice the pastry, fold back alternate long strips of pastry sitting atop the fruit and lay one of the shorter strips across the unfolded strips. Fold the long strips back over the short strip. Fold back the long strips sitting *under* the first short strip, then add a second short strip across the unfolded strips. Replace the long strips as before. Continue lifting, positioning and replacing strips in this way until the whole pie is covered with a lattice pattern.

Preheat the oven to 200°C (180°C Fan) 400°F, Gas Mark 6.

Refrigerate the pie for 20 minutes, then brush the top lattice with plant-based milk. Sprinkle with demerara sugar and bake for 70–75 minutes, or until the pastry is a rich golden brown and the fruit is bubbling. Check the pie when an hour is almost up as you might need to cover it with foil to prevent the pastry from burning.

Set aside to cool for at least 20 minutes before serving.

The pie is best served on the day it is made, but leftovers will keep for a day or two if refrigerated.

NOTE If you are not making this vegan, you can glaze the pastry with beaten egg, which will provide greater shine and browning.

RHUBARB AND CUSTARD PAVLOVA

SERVES 10

In the cold months of winter, forced rhubarb will bring a bit of brightness. Slightly sweeter than its outdoor-grown relatives, forced rhubarb is thinner and more tender, with a particularly vibrant pink colour. Of course, this can be made with any type of rhubarb.

Unsalted butter or oil, for greasing

6 large egg whites

¼ teaspoon cream of tartar

Pinch of salt

350g (12oz/1¾ cups) caster (superfine) sugar

2 teaspoons cornflour (cornstarch)

FOR THE FILLING

450g (1lb) rhubarb

100g (3½oz/½ cup) caster (superfine) sugar

Juice of 1 orange

1 teaspoon vanilla bean paste

FOR THE TOPPING

300ml (10fl oz/1¼ cups) double (heavy) cream

240ml (8½fl oz/1 cup) shop-bought custard

Preheat the oven to 180°C (160°C Fan) 350°F, Gas Mark 4.

For the filling, cut the rhubarb into 2.5cm (1in) pieces and place them in your 23 x 33cm (9 x 13in) baking tin. Sprinkle over the sugar, orange juice and vanilla and mix together briefly. Bake for 10–12 minutes, or until the rhubarb is soft and tender but still holding its shape. Carefully transfer the fruit to a bowl and set aside to cool. At this point you can either pour the juice from the tin into the bowl, or return it to the oven and continue heating until it is bubbling and slightly syrupy and then add it to the fruit. Refrigerate until needed.

Reduce the oven to 110°C (90°C Fan) 230°F, Gas Mark ¼. Wash and dry the baking tin, then lightly grease it and line with a large single sheet of parchment paper that stands slightly above all the sides.

For the pavlova, place the egg whites, cream of tartar and salt in a large bowl and whisk with an electric mixer on a medium speed until foamy, looking a little like a bubble bath. Add the sugar, a spoonful at a time, whisking well between each addition. Once all the sugar has been incorporated, continue whisking until the meringue holds stiff peaks. Add the cornflour and whisk briefly to combine. Spread the meringue inside the prepared tin, creating a depression in the middle and a higher border up the sides.

Bake for about 2 hours, or until the meringue is crisp and dry but still pale. Turn off the heat and allow it to cool in the oven for a few hours; cooling it slowly in this way helps to prevent it from cracking. (I often make the meringue on a Friday evening and leave it to cool overnight, meaning I have a ready-made dessert for the weekend. If stored in an airtight container, it will keep for a few days.)

Once the meringue is cold, use the parchment to lift it from the tin and set it on a serving platter.

For the topping, whisk the cream until it holds soft peaks, then gently fold in the custard. Spread it over the middle of the meringue and top with the roasted rhubarb.

Once assembled, this is best served on the same day.

SLAB PANCAKE

SERVES 8

I am a big fan of a brunch dish that can be whipped up quickly and still serve a crowd. This fluffy American-style pancake is great when you want something delicious for brunch but can't muster the energy to make anything more involved.

30ml (1fl oz/2 tablespoons) vegetable oil, plus extra for greasing

175g (6oz/1⅓ cups + 1 tablespoon) plain (all-purpose) flour

50g (1¾oz/¼ cup) caster (superfine) sugar

¼ teaspoon fine sea salt

1 teaspoon baking powder

½ teaspoon bicarbonate of soda (baking soda)

2 large eggs

180ml (6¼fl oz/¾ cup) whole milk

2 teaspoons vanilla extract

150g (5½oz/1 cup) blueberries

TO SERVE

Butter

Maple syrup

Preheat the oven to 190°C (170°C fan) 375°F, Gas Mark 5. Lightly grease your 23 x 33cm (9 x 13in) baking tin and line the base with parchment paper.

Place the flour, sugar, salt, baking powder and bicarbonate of soda in a large bowl and whisk to combine. Make a well in the middle and add the eggs, oil, milk and vanilla, whisking to form a smooth batter. Pour it into the prepared tin and spread evenly, then sprinkle over the blueberries.

Bake for 15–20 minutes, or until golden. Serve while still warm from the oven. Cut into slices and serve with maple syrup and butter.

The pancake is best served on the day it is made.

CHOCOLATE MOUSSE WITH MAPLE-ROASTED PEARS

SERVES 8

On my first visit to Paris when I was 18, my friends and I found ourselves at a neighbourhood brasserie speaking almost no French and on a shoestring student budget. Out of money, or maybe just full, we ordered one serving of chocolate mousse that we planned on sharing, but what arrived was a giant bowl of mousse, a ladle, several bowls and multiple spoons, the idea being that we could just help ourselves. This generosity is what baking is all about to me, so this family-style, serve-yourself chocolate mousse is my take on that memory from all those years ago.

225g (8oz) dark chocolate, 65–75% cocoa solids, roughly chopped

30g (1oz/2 tablespoons) unsalted butter

180ml (6¼fl oz/¾ cup) double (heavy) cream, plus extra, lightly whipped, to serve

6 large eggs, separated

4 tablespoons caster (superfine) sugar

FOR THE MAPLE-ROASTED PEARS

8 firm Conference or Bosc pears, peeled, cored and diced

6 tablespoons maple syrup

70g (2½oz/5 tablespoons) unsalted butter, diced

Large pinch of fine sea salt

Preheat the oven to 190ºC (170ºC Fan) 375ºF, Gas Mark 5. Start by adding the diced pears, maple syrup, butter and salt to your 23 x 33cm (9 x 13in) baking tin and stir to combine. Roast for 30–40 minutes, or until the pears are tender and lightly caramelized. Set the tin aside to cool.

For the mousse, place the chocolate in a heatproof bowl set over a pan of simmering water (ensuring the bowl doesn't touch the water) and heat, stirring occasionally, until the chocolate has fully melted. Remove the bowl from the heat and stir through the butter until melted and smooth. Set aside to cool for 5 minutes.

Lightly whisk the cream until it starts to thicken and just barely reaches soft peaks. Clean your whisk, then whisk the egg whites for a minute or so, until foamy. Slowly pour in the sugar, whisking as you do so, then continue whisking until the whites hold soft peaks.

Stir the egg yolks into the chocolate mixture. Fold in one-third of the cream until smooth. Fold in the remaining cream in two further additions. Repeat this process with the meringue.

Once you have a smooth mousse, pour it over the pears and spread evenly. Refrigerate for at least 4 hours before serving.

To serve, spoon the mousse and pears into bowls and top with a little extra lightly whipped cream.

Once made, the dessert can be refrigerated for a day, but no longer.

ETON MESS

SERVES 8

A classic British dessert, Eton mess is made with meringue, cream and strawberries, and is a quick and easy summertime dessert. This version stays close to the original idea, but uses whipped chickpea (garbanzo) liquid for the meringue, and tops it with cream, raspberries as well as strawberries, plus some chopped pistachios for texture. You can use any whippable vegan cream, but if using coconut cream, it needs to be thoroughly chilled in the can and the watery part then discarded before the creamy part is whipped.

450ml (15fl oz/1¾ cups + 2 tablespoons) whippable plant-based cream, chilled

1 teaspoon vanilla bean paste

200g (7oz) raspberries

400g (14oz) strawberries, quartered

4 tablespoons raspberry jam

4 tablespoons chopped pistachios (optional)

FOR THE MERINGUE

100ml (3½fl oz/⅓ cup + 4 teaspoons) aquafaba (canned chickpea/garbanzo liquid)

½ teaspoon cream of tartar

Pinch of salt

100g (3½oz/½ cup) caster (superfine) sugar

½ teaspoon vanilla bean paste

Preheat the oven to 110°C (90°C Fan) 230°F, Gas Mark ¼. Line the base of your 23 x 33cm (9 x 13in) baking tin with parchment paper.

To make the meringue, pour the aquafaba into a large bowl, then add the cream of tartar and salt. Using an electric mixer on a medium speed, whisk the mixture into stiff peaks. With vegan meringue it's very important to ensure the foam is strong and well established before adding the sugar, and if you're used to making traditional egg-white meringue, this will take longer than you think. The meringue should be stiff and dense, like shaving foam, and should stay put if you turn the bowl upside down. When it reaches this point, continue whisking on a medium speed as you add the sugar a spoonful at a time, ensuring each addition is well incorporated before adding the next. This is a slow process, but helps to ensure the meringues are crisp and don't become hollow when baked. Once all the sugar has been added, increase the speed and whisk until the meringue is very stiff. Add the vanilla and whisk briefly to combine.

Dollop large spoonfuls of the meringue into the prepared tin and bake for 2 hours, until dry and crisp. Turn off the heat and allow the meringues to cool slowly in the oven for a couple of hours.

To assemble the dessert, whip the cream and vanilla into soft peaks. Lift the meringues out of the tin and break into small pieces. Layer them back into the tin with the cream and fruit. Dot with small dollops of jam and finish with a sprinkling of pistachios (if using).

Once assembled, the dessert needs serving within an hour or so, as the meringue will soften when mixed with the cream.

RHUBARB AND RASPBERRY QUEEN OF PUDDINGS

SERVES 12

This classic British pudding harks back to a very different time; it's an old-fashioned way of using up leftover bread. Here stale breadcrumbs are mixed with what equate to classic custard ingredients, then baked into in a layer that is a cross between cake and custard. My version is then topped with a mixture of rhubarb and raspberry jam followed by a layer of marshmallow-like meringue. It really is a regal creation from very simple ingredients.

70g (2½oz/5 tablespoons) unsalted butter, melted and cooled, plus extra for greasing

200g (7oz) stale bread

Zest of 1 lemon

50g (1¾oz/¼ cup) caster (superfine) sugar

650ml (22fl oz/2⅔ cups + 2 teaspoons) whole milk

2 teaspoons vanilla extract

5 large egg yolks

¼ teaspoon fine sea salt

FOR THE TOPPING

4 large egg whites

200g (7oz/1 cup) caster (superfine) sugar

¼ teaspoon cream of tartar

320g (11¼oz/1 cup) jam – I use half and half raspberry and rhubarb

Preheat the oven to 180°C (160°C Fan) 350°F, Gas Mark 4. Lightly grease your 23 x 33cm (9 x 13in) baking tin and line the base with parchment paper.

Place the bread in a food processor and pulse to break it into crumbs.

Put the lemon zest and sugar in a large bowl and rub together with your fingertips until the mixture resembles wet sand. Add the butter, milk, vanilla, egg yolks and salt and whisk until combined. Tip in the breadcrumbs and stir together. Pour this mixture into the prepared tin and spread evenly.

Bake for 30–40 minutes, or until set and lightly browned. Set aside to cool for 15 minutes.

For the topping, place the egg whites, sugar and cream of tartar in a heatproof bowl and sit it over a pan of simmering water. Stir gently until the sugar has dissolved and the mixture is hot to the touch. Remove from the heat. Use an electric mixer to whisk until the meringue holds stiff peaks.

Spread the jam over the warm cake, then spread or pipe the meringue over the top.

Serve the pudding as it is, or briefly brown the meringue with a blowtorch or under a hot grill (broiler).

The dessert is best served on the day it is made.

NOTE If you wish, half the jam can be replaced with fresh raspberries.

ROASTED PINEAPPLE WITH NO-CHURN COCONUT ICE CREAM

SERVES 4

No-churn ice cream is a genius invention, a mixture of just cream and condensed milk, it's simplicity itself to make. This vegan version uses the same idea but with non-dairy ingredients – whipped coconut cream and coconut condensed milk. The flavour, with the addition of lime, is surprisingly refreshing, and perfect served with sticky roasted pineapple.

2 x 400ml (14fl oz) cans full-fat coconut milk, chilled overnight

320g (11¼oz) can coconut condensed milk

Zest and juice of 1 lime

1 teaspoon vanilla bean paste

2 tablespoons light brown sugar

FOR THE ROASTED PINEAPPLE

1 large pineapple

Zest and juice of 1 lime

30g (1oz/2 tablespoons) vegan butter

75g (2¾oz/⅓ cup) light brown sugar

The ice cream needs to freeze for at least 4 hours before it is served, so prepare it ahead. Open the chilled coconut milk, which will have separated, and carefully discard the water. Scoop the cream into a large bowl, then add the condensed milk, lime zest and juice, the vanilla and sugar. Using an electric mixer, whisk until the mixture just starts to hold soft peaks. Scrape into a lidded plastic container and freeze for at least 4 hours.

Preheat the oven to 190ºC (170ºC Fan) 375ºF, Gas Mark 5.

Carefully slice the top and bottom off the pineapple, then cut it in half lengthways. Cut each half into wedges, then remove the core section and trim off the skin. Place the fruit in your 23 x 33cm (9 x 13in) baking tin, scatter over the lime zest and juice, and dot with the butter. Finish by sprinkling over the sugar.

Roast for about 30 minutes, flipping the pineapple occasionally, until it is lightly caramelized and the liquid is slightly syrupy.

Serve the pineapple and its syrup while still warm, with a scoop of the coconut ice cream.

Kept frozen, the ice cream will keep for about a week. The pineapple, if stored in a sealed container and refrigerated, will keep for a couple of days.

MACAROON COCONUT CREAM PIE

SERVES 12

Coconut cream pie has always been a favourite of mine, but let's be real – sometimes you just can't be bothered to make pastry. This version of the classic pie uses a macaroon base for both ease and flavour. It can be made in minutes and magically holds its shape in the tin without shrinking or slumping, plus it gives a great chewy texture to the dish. Traditionally, I would mix some coconut through the custard filling, but with the macaroon base, this would be coconut overload, even for me. Instead, the custard is made with coconut milk for a rich, creamy coconut flavour.

400ml (14fl oz) can full-fat coconut milk

120ml (4fl oz/½ cup) double (heavy) cream

3 large eggs

200g (7oz/1 cup) caster (superfine) sugar

50g (1¾oz/6 tablespoons) cornflour (cornstarch)

2 teaspoons vanilla bean paste

½ teaspoon coconut extract (optional)

FOR THE MACAROON PIE CRUST

250g (9oz/3 cups) desiccated coconut

150g (5½oz/¾ cup) caster (superfine) sugar

45g (1½oz/⅓ cup) gluten-free flour

Pinch of fine sea salt

3 large egg whites

FOR THE TOPPING

480ml (17fl oz/2 cups) double (heavy) cream

2 tablespoons desiccated coconut

Zest of 1 lime (optional)

Place the coconut milk and cream in a large saucepan and bring to a simmer. Meanwhile, put the eggs, sugar, cornflour and vanilla in a large bowl and whisk until smooth. Once the milk is at a simmer, pour it over the egg mixture, whisking as you pour to prevent the eggs from scrambling. Pour the custard back into the pan and whisk over a medium heat until the mixture thickens and starts to bubble. Transfer immediately to a bowl, add the coconut extract (if using), then press a sheet of clingfilm (plastic wrap) directly onto the surface of the custard and refrigerate until chilled.

Preheat the oven to 180°C (160°C Fan) 350°F, Gas Mark 4. Lightly grease your 23 x 33cm (9 x 13in) baking tin and line with a strip of parchment paper that overhangs the long sides, securing it with metal clips.

For the crust, put all the ingredients into a bowl and mix until thoroughly combined. Scrape into the prepared tin and press evenly over the base and slightly up the sides. Bake for 25–30 minutes, or until golden brown. Set aside to cool. Once cooled, use the parchment paper to carefully lift the crust out of the tin.

Beat the chilled custard until smooth, then pour it into the pie crust and spread evenly.

For the topping, lightly whisk the cream until it holds soft peaks, then spread it over the custard. Sprinkle with the coconut and lime zest (if using).

The custard can be made a couple of days in advance, but the base is best made and served on the day it is made because after that it will start to soften.

SOUR CHERRY CROISSANT BREAD PUDDING

SERVES 10

If you're the sort of person who hates bread pudding because it's so often kind of mushy and a bit bland, this version is for you. Stale croissants are chopped up and soaked with custard that is flavoured with vanilla and just a touch of almond extract, and studded with sour cherries. The texture comes from the fact that the tops of the croissants are added on top of the pudding. They soak up some custard, but they remain crisp as they bake and add a wonderful crunchy element to the dish, which is pleasingly soft and tender underneath.

Butter, for greasing

8 stale croissants

200g (7oz) sour cherries, pitted if fresh, defrosted if frozen

375ml (12¾fl oz/1½ cups + 1 tablespoon) whole milk

375ml (12¾fl oz/1½ cups + 1 tablespoon) double (heavy) cream

5 large eggs

50g (1¾oz/¼ cup) caster (superfine) sugar

1 teaspoon vanilla bean paste

1 teaspoon almond extract

FOR THE TOPPING

Demerara sugar

1–2 tablespoons flaked (sliced) almonds

Lightly grease your 23 x 33cm (9 x 13in) baking tin with a little butter.

Slice all the croissants in half horizontally, setting 6 of the top halves aside. Cut the remaining croissant pieces into small chunks and add to the prepared tin. Add about three-quarters of the cherries and mix well.

Combine the milk, cream, eggs, sugar, vanilla and almond extract in a large bowl and whisk together. Pour this custard over the croissants.

Arrange the reserved croissant tops over the pudding, lightly pressing them into the custard to help them soak up the liquid. Scatter over the remaining cherries, then set the pudding aside for about 30 minutes, gently pressing down on the croissants every now and then, and spooning a little custard over the croissant tops.

Preheat the oven to 170ºC (150ºC Fan) 325ºF, Gas Mark 3.

Sprinkle liberally with demerara sugar and scatter over the flaked almonds. Bake for 40–45 minutes, or until the custard is puffed up and set. Keep an eye on the pudding as it bakes, and if the croissants are browning too quickly, tent the tin with foil. Allow to cool slightly before serving with a little cream.

Bread pudding is best served on the day it is made, but leftovers will keep for a couple of days if refrigerated, and can be served cold or gently rewarmed in the oven.

169

RESOURCES

THE TIN

Divertimenti
www.divertimenti.co.uk

Nordic Ware
www.nordicware.com

GENERAL BAKEWARE

Divertimenti
www.divertimenti.co.uk

John Lewis
www.johnlewis.com

Williams Sonoma
www.williams-sonoma.com
www.williams-sonoma.com.au

GLUTEN-FREE FLOUR

Doves Farm
www.dovesfarm.co.uk

Bob's Red Mill
www.bobsredmill.com

TAHINI

Belazu
www.belazu.co.uk

Seed + Mill
www.seedandmill.com

VANILLA PRODUCTS

Heilala Vanilla
www.heilalavanilla.com
www.amazon.co.uk

VEGAN BUTTER

Naturli'
www.naturli-foods.com

Miyoko's
www.miyokos.com

INDEX

ABOUT THE AUTHOR

Edd Kimber is is a baker and food writer based in London. He is the author of *The Boy Who Bakes* (2011), *Say it with Cake* (2012), *Patisserie Made Simple* (2014) and *One Tin Bakes* (2020). Over the last ten years he has appeared on multiple television shows including *Good Morning America*, *The Alan Titchmarsh Show*, *Sunday Brunch*, *Saturday Kitchen* and, of course, on the original series of *The Great British Bake Off*, of which he is the inaugural winner.

He regularly shares his knowledge at cookery schools and at food festivals around the world and also writes for multiple publications, including as the baking columnist for *Olive* magazine.

@THEBOYWHOBAKES
WWW.THEBOYWHOBAKES.CO.UK

ACKNOWLEDGMENTS

Thanks to everyone at Kyle Books, especially Louise and Judith; I have loved writing these recipes and this book and I am extremely proud of the end result and cannot wait to see people baking from it.

Thanks to my agent Katherine for always understanding what I want and where I want my career to go.

Thanks to Shauna and Erin, two excellent bakers who each inspired a recipe in the book.

Thanks to Mike who allowed me to take over our kitchen 24/7 and tried everything and was always honest with his feedback.

My biggest thanks though has to go to the readers of the original *One Tin Bakes*. That first volume came out in the middle of a global pandemic, in the midst of a national lockdown. Baking seemed to capture the world's attention and *One Tin Bakes* became one of the books so many people enjoyed baking from and really took to their hearts. The messages I received from readers all around the world really gave me something to feel proud about and really helped me get through a tough year. The success of that book also allowed me to write this follow up and I hope this book gives you as much pleasure as the first.

Sweet and simple traybakes, pies, bars and buns

Edd Kimber

ONE TIN BAKES

'Kimber can't help his jazz hands: His creative dial is set to 11.' NEW YORK TIMES

'A dazzler of a baking book.' DAN LEPARD

'I love a sheet cake and the generosity in these recipes makes me want to go to a picnic or a potluck.' CLAIRE PTAK

'An absolute must-have for every home baker.' JOY WILSON

'A terrifically clever idea.' HELEN GOH

'Simple, creative, perfectly-executed.' THE SMITTEN KITCHEN

'Baking requires skill and perfection and Edd's got it.' MARY BERRY